Beginning to Pray

Anthony Bloom

Since *Beginning to Pray* was first published in 1970, it has established itself as a modern spiritual classic. Hailed by both Catholics and Protestants, it was written by an Orthodox Archbishop for people who had never prayed before and has been read and loved by persons at all levels of spiritual development.

"The realm of God is dangerous," says the author. "You must enter into it and not just seek information about it. . . . The day when God is absent, when he is silent—that is the beginning of prayer."

BEGINNING TO PRAY

**Large Print Inspirational Books
from
Walker**

Would you like to be on our
Large Print mailing list?

Please send your
name and address to:

Beth Walker
Walker and Company
720 Fifth Avenue
New York, NY 10019

BEGINNING TO PRAY

Anthony Bloom

Phoenix Press

WALKER AND COMPANY
New York

Large Print Edition published by arrangement with Paulist Press

Originally published under the title
School for Prayer by
Darton, Longman & Todd Ltd.,
London, England, © 1970.

Copyright © 1970 by
Archbishop Anthony Bloom

Printed in the United States of America.

Library of Congress Cataloging in Publication Data

Bloom, Anthony, 1914–
　　Beginning to pray.

　　1. Prayer. 2. Spiritual life—Orthodox Eastern authors. 3. Bloom, Anthony, 1914–　　—Interviews.
4. Large type books. I. Title.
[BV210.2.B578 1986]　　248.3　　85-20254
ISBN 0-8027-2517-1 (lg. print)

First Large Print Edition, 1986
Walker and Company
720 Fifth Avenue
New York, NY 10019

CONTENTS

INTRODUCTION

Interview With Archbishop Anthony Bloom

by
Timothy Wilson

T.W.: Were you born in Russia?

Bloom: I was born in Switzerland in fact, because my father was a diplomat and happened to be there when I was born. But we returned to Russia just before the First World War.

T.W.: What happened after that?

Bloom: My father went to serve in the Orient, in Persia, and that's where I spent the second part of my childhood.

T. W.: What happened to your family after the Russian Revolution?

Bloom: We crossed the north of Persia on horseback and in horse-driven carts, then over the mountains of Kurdistan, then down the Tigris and the Euphrates in a barge. We ended up in a small English boat going to India and from there we got a boat going towards Southampton. I say "towards" because in fact we never arrived. Just as we were setting off we were told that the boat was far too old to weather any storm so I was full of hopes—that I would end up as a kind of Robinson Crusoe marooned on a desert island. I could never understand how my mother could be so unromantic as to hope for good weather, but anyhow God happened to be on the side of the grown-ups and in the end we landed safely at Gibraltar. But the boat couldn't go any farther. So part of our luggage went on to Southampton—we got it back about fourteen years later and had to pay a pound for customs. Meanwhile we travelled through Spain, France, Austria and then into Yugoslavia. Eventually we came back to Austria where I went to school for a while, then back into France in 1923. And we finally settled there for the next twenty-seven years or so.

T.W.: This is a very exciting and romantic childhood. But what happened to your father? What sort of job did he do?

Bloom: Of course, he had left the diplomatic service and he decided to make a complete end to the past. He decided to take upon himself responsibility for all the tragic developments which had taken place in Russia and so he became, by choice, an unskilled workman. He worked on the railways, in factories, and did that kind of work until his health gave way. Then he turned to clerical work. But he never tried to readjust himself to the old standards, because he felt that the past was the past and one should take responsibility for all that had happened in Russia.

T.W.: Your father seems to have been an extraordinary man. Can you remember very much about him?

Bloom: I remember a certain number of his

phrases. In fact there are two things he said which impressed me and have stayed with me all my life. One is about life. I remember he said to me after a holiday, "I worried about you" and I said, "Did you think I'd had an accident?" He said, "That would have meant nothing, even if you had been killed. I thought you had lost your integrity." Then on another occasion he said to me, "Always remember that whether you are alive or dead matters nothing. What matters is what you live for and what you are prepared to die for." These things were the background of my early education and show the sense of life that I got from him.

T.W.: What happened about your own education during this period?

Bloom: After going to school in the normal way, I began to work when I was twelve—giving lessons to children who were younger than I so that I could pay for the books that I needed at school.

T.W.: What did you teach?

Bloom: Arithmetic and anything which I already knew and they didn't. Later on I taught Latin which I knew very well and managed to pay my way through university by working in this way. I would give three or four hours of lessons every evening, teaching physics, chemistry and Latin and this gave me enough money to live on while I was studying.

T.W.: It must have been a very hard life.

Bloom: Yes, it meant that I couldn't do any of my own work on week-day evenings and so I had to cram it all into the weekends, which often meant working all through the night. I used to go to bed at eight in the morning and sleep until midday, then start working again. It nearly finished me, but at least it enabled me to carry on with my studies.

T.W.: Were you studying medicine at this time?

Bloom: After secondary school where I read classics, I went to the School of Science at the Sorbonne and studied physics, chemistry and biology. After graduating (from there) I went to medical school where I finished in 1939 just as the war broke out.

T.W.: So you were qualified as a doctor in 1939?

Bloom: Yes. But then I was called up, in September 1939, and I became involved in the war in two ways—at the beginning and the end I was in the French army doing surgery and during the middle part of the war I was in the French resistance.

T.W.: You were working in a French hospital during the German occupation?

Bloom: I worked for some time in the hospital, but at a certain moment it became risky because I had joined the resistance and we had been doing resistance work there. So I left and taught in a school for a while.

T.W.: You were never caught.

Bloom: No, I'm afraid I never managed to be a hero even in that way.

T.W.: What was your nationality?

Bloom: Up until 1937 I was stateless, but in 1937 I applied for French nationality and I have kept it right until now. So technically I am French, but I belong to that generation which is Russian at heart. By education, culture and so on I can't feel that I belong completely to one side or the other. In Russia I feel Russian because it's my language, it's my country—yet I don't belong to it because I am an émigré. Abroad I am much too Russian to be able to melt completely into the milieu around me.

T.W.: When did you become a Christian? Was there any particular turning point?

Bloom: It came in several stages. Up to my middle teens I was an unbeliever and very aggressively anti-church. I knew no God, I wasn't interested and hated everything that connected with the idea of God.

T.W.: In spite of your father?

Bloom: Yes, because up to the age of 15

life had been very hard, we had no common roof and I was at boarding school which was rough and violent. All the members of my family lived in different corners of Paris. It was only when I was about 14 that we all gathered under a common roof and that was real happiness and bliss—it is odd to think that in a suburban house in Paris one could discover perfect happiness but it was so. This was the first time that we had had a home since the revolution. But before that I ought to say that I had met something which puzzled me a great deal. I was sent to a boys' summer camp when I was about eleven years old and there I met a priest who must have been about thirty. Something about him struck me—he had love to spare for everyone and his love wasn't conditioned by whether we were good and it never changed when we were bad. It was an unconditional ability to love. I had never met this in my life before. I had been loved at home, but I found it natural. I had friends too and that was natural, but I had never met this kind of love. At the time I didn't trace it to anything, I just found this man extremely puzzling and extremely lovable. Only years later, when I had already discovered the Gospel, did it occur to me that he loved with a love that was beyond him. He shared out divine love to us, or if you prefer, his human love was of such depth and had such scope and scale that he could include all of us, either through joy or pain, but still within our love. This experience I think was the first deep spiritual experience I had.

T.W.: What happened after this?

Bloom: Nothing. I went back to boarding school and everything went on as before until we all found ourselves under the same roof. When I found myself confronted with perfect happiness, a quite unexpected thing happened. I suddenly discovered that if happiness is aimless, it's unbearable. I could not accept aimless happiness. Hardships and suffering had to be overcome, there was always something beyond them. But because it had no further meaning and because I believed in nothing, happiness seemed to be stale. So I decided I would give myself a year to see whether life had any meaning. If in the course of that year

I could not find any meaning, I decided I would not live, I would commit suicide.

T.W.: How did you get out of this aimless happiness?

Bloom: I began to look for a meaning in life other than what I could find through purposefulness. Studying and making oneself useful for life didn't convince me at all. All my life up to now had been concentrated on immediate goals, and suddenly these became empty. I felt something immensely dramatic inside myself, and everything around me seemed small and meaningless.

Months passed and no meaning appeared on the horizon. One day—it was during Lent, and I was then a member of one of the Russian youth organisations in Paris—one of the leaders came up to me and said, "We have invited a priest to talk to you. Come." I answered with violent indignation that I would not. I had no use for the Church. I did not believe in God. I did not want to waste any of my time. The leader was subtle—he explained that everyone who belonged to my group had reacted in exactly the same way, and if no one came we would all be put to shame because the priest had come and we would be disgraced if no one attended his talk. "Don't listen" the leader said. "I don't care, but just sit and be a physical presence." That much loyalty I was prepared to give to my youth organisation, so I sat through the lecture. I didn't intend to listen. But my ears pricked up. I became more and more indignant. I saw a vision of Christ and Christianity that was profoundly repulsive to me. When the lecture was over I hurried home in order to check the truth of what he had been saying. I asked my mother whether she had a book of the Gospel, because I wanted to know whether the Gospel would support the monstrous impression I had derived from his talk. I expected nothing good from my reading, so I counted the chapters of the four Gospels to be sure I read the shortest, not to waste time unnecessarily. I started to read St. Mark's Gospel.

While I was reading the beginning of St. Mark's Gospel, before I reached the third chapter, I suddenly became aware that on the other side of my desk there was a presence. And the certainty was so strong that it was Christ standing there that it has never left me. This was the real turning point. Because Christ was alive and I had been in his presence I could say with certainty that what the Gospel said about the crucifixion of the prophet of Galilee was true, and the centurion was right when he said, "Truly he is the Son of God". It was in the light of the Resurrection that I could read with certainty the story of the Gospel, knowing that everything was true in it because the impossible event of the Resurrection was to me more certain than any event of history. History I had to believe, the Resurrection I knew for a fact. I did not discover, as you see, the Gospel beginning with its first message of the Annunciation, and it did not unfold for me as a story which one can believe or disbelieve. It began as an event that left all problems of disbelief behind because it was a direct and personal experience.

T.W.: And this conviction has stayed with you all through your life? There have been no times when you have doubted your faith?

Bloom: I became absolutely certain within myself that Christ is alive and that certain things existed. I didn't have all the answers, but having touched that experience, I was certain that ahead of me there were answers, visions, possibilities. This is what I mean by faith—not doubting in the sense of being in confusion and perplexity, but doubting in order to discover the reality of the life, the kind of doubt that makes you want to question and discover more, that makes you want to explore.

T.W.: When were you ordained?

Bloom: I was ordained in 1948 but before that I took monastic vows. This was done secretly because it was incompatible to openly profess monastic vows and also to be a physician. So I lived a sort of monastic life under the cover of my medical work, trying to be inwardly faithful to stability, to poverty, to chastity, to obedience, but expressing all these things in my medical situation—whether in the war, or afterwards during peacetime when I became a general practitioner. Then when I became a priest the fact that I had taken vows came out into the open. Nowadays we lack priests to such an extent that none of my generation who became monks with the intention of leading a secluded or retiring life was given a chance to do it. We were all called by our bishops and sent out into pastoral work.

T.W.: You are still a monk . . .

Bloom: Yes.

T.W.: But you are, so to speak, living in the market place.

Bloom: I don't think living in the market place is any different from living in the wilderness. To be poor financially is in a way much easier than to be poor inwardly, to have no attachments. This is very difficult to learn and something which happens gradually, from year to year. You really learn to value things, to look at people and see the radiant beauty which they possess—without the desire to possess them. To pluck a flower means to take possession of it, and it also means to kill it. The vow of poverty makes me appreciate things much more. But first of all one must learn to be free within oneself. There are moments when you must physically absent yourself in order to learn what it means for something or somebody to exist in his own right and not just as a mirror of your own emotions.

So often when we say "I love you" we say it with a huge "I" and a small "you". We use love as a conjunction instead of it being a verb implying action. It's no good just gazing out into open space hoping to see the Lord; instead we have to look closely at our neighbour, someone whom God has willed into existence, someone whom God has died for. Everyone we meet has a right to exist, because he has value in himself, and we are not used to this. The acceptance of otherness is a danger to us, it threatens us. To recognise the other's right to be himself might mean recognising his right to kill me. But if we set a limit to his right to exist, it's no right at all. Love is difficult. Christ was crucified because he taught a kind of love which is a terror for men, a love which demands total surrender: it spells death.

T.W.: What do you mean by that?

Bloom: If we turn to God and come face to face with Him, we must be prepared to pay the cost. If we are not prepared to pay the cost, we must walk through life being a beggar, hoping someone else will pay. But if we turn to God we discover that life is deep, vast and immensely worth living.

T.W.: Can we go back to the time when you were secretly a monk and also a doctor? What did you learn from this experience?

Bloom: I will give you one practical example. In the hospital where I was working as a war surgeon, a German came in once with one finger smashed by a bullet. The head surgeon came round and looked at the finger and said "Take it off". That was a very quick and easy decision—it would take only five minutes to do. Then the German said, "Is there anyone here who can speak German?" I spoke with the man and discovered that he was a watchmaker and if his finger was removed he would probably never be able to work again. So we spent five weeks treating his smashed finger and he was able to leave the hospital with five fingers instead of only four. From this I learnt that the fact that he was a watchmaker was as important as anything else. I would say that I learnt to put human concerns first. Then one began to pray—a stable prayer, standing before God, face to face, and simply being with God.

T.W.: Then after being ordained you came to Britain?

Bloom: I came to Britain at the end of January 1949 to be chaplain of the Anglican-Orthodox fellowship of St. Alban and Sergius, which may sound rather daring considering that I knew not a word of English at that time.

T.W.: I don't suppose it took you very long to learn English.

Bloom: To learn the sort of basic English that allowed me to communicate—and to communicate also a great deal of fun and laughter at my expense—that didn't take long.

T.W.: Do you find any difficulty in communicating now? After all, the Christian faith is not something which people can easily or readily understand.

Bloom: I don't find it a problem. What I aim at is to live within a situation and to be totally engrossed in it and yet free from involvement. The basic thing is that I never ask myself what the result of any action will be—that is God's concern. The only question I keep asking myself in life is: what should I do at this particular moment? What should I say? All you can do is to be at every single moment as true as you can with all the power in your being—and then leave it to God to use you, even despite yourself.

Whenever I speak I speak with all the conviction and belief which is in me. I stake my life on what I am saying. It's not the words themselves that are important but reaching down to the level of people's convictions. This is the basis of communication, this is where we really meet one another. If people want to ridicule me, that's fine; but if it produces a spark in them and we can talk, then it means we are really talking about something which concerns us deeply.

T.W.: Do you find that the surface culture of the modern English way of life makes it difficult to communicate the Gospel?

Bloom: Yes, because the Gospel must reach not only the intellect but the whole being. English people often say, "That's interesting, let's talk about it, let's explore it as an idea," but actually do nothing about it. To meet God means to enter into the "cave of a tiger"—it is not a pussy cat you meet—it's a tiger. The realm of God is dangerous. You must enter into it and not just seek information about it.

T.W.: Was there anything in particular which struck you about England when you came here?

Bloom: When I arrived in England I was appalled at the British attitude to death. To die seemed to be almost an act of indecency

—if you had fallen so low as to die, then there were special people who would come, undertakers, to pack and wrap you up for the funeral. Then two weeks or so later there is a nice memorial service in which one sublimates one's feelings into a kind of spiritual realm. Then I remember that I went to preach at the University Church in Cambridge on the subject of death and a priest there told me he had never seen a dead person. Why is there this morbid attitude to death? In a natural way one does not get rid of people through the back door! If death is nothing but defeat, the end of life, it is not pleasant for the family to look and think it will happen to them soon. Of course, if you have a wrong attitude to death, it becomes more and more horrible and frightening. I remember another incident. An old lady died and the family telephoned me and asked me to come because I was a friend. I arrived but could see no sign of the children. I asked why they weren't there, because in the Orthodox Church the children always go to the dead person and the coffin is left open. The mother said, "They will be terrified, they know what death is." It turned out that quite recently the children had seen a dead rabbit which had been crushed by a car, and the parents thought they would be frightened if they saw granny. I asked if the children could come in, otherwise, I said to the parents, they might always have this frightened attitude to death. Eventually the parents agreed to let the children come into the house and we went up to the room where granny was lying. We stood beside the bed in silence for a while then one of the children said, "How beautiful granny looks". Death was no longer something frightening, something to be dreaded.

T.W.: You haven't said anything about your mother, but I believe she was very close to you.

Bloom: She was a marvellous woman, very simple and direct. My own experience of death came through my mother because she had cancer. Life acquired a tremendous significance—everything we said or did could have been a last gesture, everything had to embody forty years of love.

T.W.: Being an émigré and having this

feeling of not really belonging must have made a difference to you. Looking back on your life, would you say that your Christian faith was influenced by this experience?

Bloom: I think this is true. During the Revolution we lost the Christ of the great cathedrals, the Christ of the splendidly architected liturgies; and we discovered the Christ who is vulnerable just as we're vulnerable, we discovered the Christ who was rejected just as we were rejected, and we discovered the Christ who had nothing at His moment of crisis, not even friends, and this was similar to our experience.

God helps us when there is no one else to help. God is there at the point of greatest tension, at the breaking point, at the centre of the storm. In a way despair is at the centre of things—if only we are prepared to go through it. We must be prepared for a period when God is not there for us and we must be aware of not trying to substitute a false God. One day, as I described in the book, a girl came to my surgery and condemned the Gospels without having read them. On her honeymoon she went to the cinema with her husband and she suddenly went blind. Later they discovered that she had an incurable disease. In the final stages of her illness she wrote to me, "My heart hasn't the strength to beat Godwards" and she had the courage to accept real absence and would not substitute a false God, a comforter. The tremendous courage of this person impressed me immensely and I have never forgotten that.

The day when God is absent, when He is silent—that is the beginning of prayer. Not when we have a lot to say, but when we say to God "I can't live without You, why are You so cruel, so silent?" This knowledge that we must find or die—that makes us break through to the place where we are in the Presence. If we listen to what our hearts know of love and longing and are never afraid of despair, we find that victory is always there the other side of it.

And there is that time when there is a longing in the heart for God Himself, not for His gifts, but for God Himself. There is sadness in the eyes that grow deep and look into infinity, often in the midst of fulfilment and happiness. There is longing for home, but a home that has no geography, home where there is love, depth and life.

T.W.: I remember you saying "I am mad, but it is an odd kind of madness because other people want to catch it". What did you mean by that?

Bloom: As Christians we are always in tension—in anguish and at the same time in bliss. This is mad, ridiculous. But it is true—accepting the dark night just as we accept the brilliance of the day. We have to make an act of surrender—if I am in Christ, there are moments when I must share the cry of the Lord on the cross and the anguish in the garden of Gethsemane. There is a way of being defeated, even in our faith—and this is a way of sharing the anguish of the Lord. I don't believe that we should ever say, "This cannot happen to you". If we are Christians we should go through this life, accepting the life and the world, not trying to create a falsified world.

But, on the other hand, the Christian is like someone who lives in three dimensions in a world in which the majority of people live in two. People who live freely and

24

within a dimension of eternity will always find that something is wrong, they will always find themselves being the odd man out. The same problem was faced by the early Christians when they said that their only king was God. People turned round to them and said, "If you say that you are disloyal to our king" and often persecuted them. But the only true way of being loyal to this two-dimensional world is to be loyal to the three-dimensional world, because in reality the world is three-dimensional. If you really live in three dimensions and do not simply live in two and imagine the third, then life will be full and meaningful. The early Christians were able to do it and Christians today are also able to do that.

T.W.: I'd like to ask you one final question —about Russia. You go there quite often. What happens?

Bloom: I go to Russia once a year to report to the Patriarch about church life in western Europe, to lecture in the theological colleges and also to keep in touch with the Russian Church. I celebrate there,

I preach in the churches and I talk to ordinary people.

T.W.: Do you get politically involved?

Bloom: What we have tried to achieve is a creative tension between belonging unreservedly to the Church of Russia and asserting that we are political émigrés. In the position of tension in which we are, between churchmanship and citizenship, our churchmanship is much freer than if we had a better harmony between Church and State.

T.W.: How much active religion is there in Russia today?

Bloom: I think there is a great deal of it. Statistically we would reckon that we have about thirty million churchgoers in Russia, which is a large number after fifty years of systematic eradication of the faith in the Stalin period by extreme violence and then systematic propaganda. But in fact young people in Russia have become increasingly interested in matters of the spiritual life, and there is an increasing number of young people who come to church, either to investigate or to remain members of it. There is a vast circle of young people who belong to this realm in which God, spiritual matters, are of great importance.

T.W.: There is a sense when you speak, I don't mean when you talk of Russia, but in general, of making huge demands of people. You talked earlier about "paying the cost" and you have this feeling about death not really being important.

Bloom: I think this is true. Perhaps I can illustrate this from a story taken from the late history of the Russian Church. I think it shows what I am trying to say about being a Christian. In the years of the Civil War when the opposing armies were contending for power, conquering and losing ground in the course of three years, a small town fell into the hands of the Red army which had been held by the remnants of the Imperial troops. A woman found herself there with her two small children, four and five years of age, in danger of death because her husband belonged to the opposite camp. She hid in an abandoned house hoping that the time would come when she would be able to escape. One evening a young woman, Natalie, of her own age, in the early twenties, knocked at the door and asked her whether she was so-and-so. When the mother said she was, the young woman warned her that she had been discovered and would be fetched that very night in order to be shot. The young woman added, "You must escape at once." The mother looked at the children and said, "How could I?" The young woman, who thus far had been nothing but a physical neighbour, became at that moment the neighbour of the Gospel. She said, "You can, because I will stay behind and call myself by your name when they come to fetch you." "But you will be shot," said the mother. "Yes, but I have no children." And she stayed behind.

We can imagine what happened then. We can see the night coming, wrapping in darkness, in gloom, in cold and damp, this cottage. We can see there a woman who was waiting for her death to come and we can remember the Garden of Gethsemane. We can imagine Natalie asking that this cup should pass her by and being met like

Christ by divine silence. We can imagine her turning in intention towards those who might have supported her, but who were out of reach. The disciples of Christ slept; and she could turn to no one without betraying. We can imagine that more than once she prayed that at least her sacrifice should not be in vain.

Natalie probably asked herself more than once what would happen to the mother and the children when she was dead, and there was no reply except the word of Christ, "No one has greater love than he who lays down his life for his friend." Probably she thought more than once that in one minute she could be secure! It was enough to open the door and the moment she was in the street she no longer was that woman, she became herself again. It was enough to deny her false, her shared identity. But she died, shot. The mother and the children escaped.

THE ABSENCE OF GOD

As we start learning to pray, I would like to make it clear that what I mean by "learning to pray" is not an attempt to justify or explain this in a speculative way. Rather, I would like to point out what one should be aware of, and what one can do if one wishes to pray. As I am a beginner myself, I will assume that you are also beginners, and we will try to begin together. I am not speaking to anyone who aims at mystical prayer or higher states of perfection, because these things will teach themselves. When God breaks through to us or when we break through to God, in certain exceptional circumstances, either because things suddenly disclose themselves with a depth we have never before perceived or when we suddenly discover in ourselves a depth where prayer abides and out of which it can gush forth, there is no problem of prayer. When we are aware of God, we stand before Him, worship Him, speak to Him.

At the outset there is, then, one very important problem: the situation of one for whom God seems to be absent. This is what I would like to speak about now. Obviously I am not speaking of a real absence—God is never really absent—but of the *sense* of absence which we have. We stand before God and we shout into an empty sky, out of which there is no reply. We turn in all directions and He is not to be found. What ought we to think of this situation?

First of all, it is very important to remember that prayer is an encounter and a relationship, a relationship which is deep, and this relationship cannot be forced either on us or on God. The fact that God can make Himself present or can leave us with the sense of His absence is part of this live and real relationship. If we could mechanically draw Him into an encounter, force Him to meet us, simply because we have chosen this moment to meet Him, there would be no relationship and no encounter. We can do that with an image, with the imagination, or with the various idols we can put in front of us instead of God; we can do nothing of the sort with the living God, any more than we can do it with a living person. A relationship must begin and develop in mutual freedom. If you look at the relationship in terms of *mutual* relationship, you will see that God could complain about us a great deal more than we about Him. We complain that He does not make Himself present to us for the few minutes we reserve for Him, but what about the twenty-three and a half hours during which God may be knocking at our door and we answer "I am busy, I am sorry" or when we do not answer at all because we do not even hear the knock at the door of our heart, of our minds, of our conscience, of our life. So there is a situation in which we have no right to complain of the absence of God, because we are a great deal more absent than He ever is.

The second very important thing is that a meeting face to face with God is always a moment of judgment for us. We cannot meet God in prayer or in meditation or in contemplation and not be either saved or condemned. I do not mean this in major terms of eternal damnation or eternal salvation already given and received, but it is always a critical moment, a crisis. "Crisis" comes from the Greek and means "judgment". To meet God face to face in prayer is a critical moment in our lives, and thanks be to Him that He does not always present Himself to us when we wish to meet Him, because we might not be able to endure such a meeting. Remember the many passages in Scripture in which we are told how bad it is to find oneself face to face with God, because God is power, God is truth, God is purity. Therefore, the first thought we ought to have when we do not tangibly perceive the divine presence, is a thought of gratitude. God is merciful; He does not come in an untimely way. He gives us a chance to judge ourselves, to understand, and not to come into His presence at a moment when it would mean condemnation.

I would like to give you an example of this. Many years ago a man came to see me. He asked me to show him God. I told him I could not but I added that even if I could, he would not be able to see Him, because I thought—and I do think—that to meet God one must have something in common with Him, something that gives you eyes to see, perceptiveness to perceive. He asked me then why I thought as I did, and I suggested that he should think a few moments and tell me whether there was any passage in the Gospel that moved him particularly, to see what was the connection between him and God. He said "Yes, in the eighth chapter of the Gospel according to St. John, the passage concerning the woman taken in adultery." I said, "Good, this is one of the most beautiful and moving passages. Now sit back and ask yourself, who are you in the scene which is described? Are you the Lord, or at least on His side, full of mercy, of understanding and full of faith in this woman who can repent and become a new creature? Are you the woman taken in adultery? Are you one of the older men who walk out at once because they are aware of their own sins, or one of the young ones who wait?" He thought for a few minutes then said "No, I feel I am the only Jew who would not have walked out but who would have stoned the woman." I said "Thank God that He does not allow you to meet Him face to face."

This may be an extreme example, but how often could we recognise similar situations in ourselves? Not that we flatly refuse God's word or God's example, but that in a less violent way we do what the soldiers did during the Passion. We would love to cover Christ's eyes, to be able to deal Him blows freely without being seen. Do we not do this, to a certain extent, when we ignore the divine presence and act according to our own desires, our moods, contrary to everything which is God's will? We try to blind Him, but in fact we blind ourselves. At such moments, how can we come into His presence? We can indeed, in repentance, broken-hearted; but we cannot come in the way in which we immediately wish to be received—with love, with friendship.

Look at the various passages in the Gospel. People much greater than ourselves hesitated to receive Christ. Remember the centurion who asked Christ to heal his servant. Christ said "I will come", but the centurion said "No, don't. Say a word and he will be healed." Do we do that? Do we turn to God and say "Don't make Yourself tangibly, perceptively present before me. It is enough for You to say a word and I will be healed. It is enough for You to say a word and things *will* happen. I do not need more for the moment." Or take Peter in his boat after the great catch of fish, when he fell on his knees and said "Leave me, O Lord, I am a sinner." He asked the Lord to leave his boat because he felt humble—and he felt humble because he had suddenly perceived the greatness of Jesus. Do we ever do that? When we read the Gospel and the image of Christ becomes compelling, glorious, when we pray and we become aware of the greatness, the holiness of God, do we ever say "I am unworthy that He should come near me?" Not to speak of all the occasions when we should be aware that He cannot come to us because we are not there to receive Him. We want something *from* Him, not *Him* at all. Is that a relationship? Do we behave in that way with our friends? Do we aim at what friendship can *give* us or is it the friend whom we love? Is this true with regard to the Lord?

Let us think of our prayers, yours and mine; think of the warmth, the depth and intensity of your prayer when it concerns someone you love or something which matters to your life. Then your heart is open, all your inner self is recollected in the prayer. Does it mean that God matters to you? No, it does not. It simply means that the subject matter of your prayer matters to you. For when you have made your passionate, deep, intense prayer concerning the person you love or the situation that worries you, and you turn to the next item, which does not matter so much —if you suddenly grow cold, what has changed? Has God grown cold? Has He gone? No, it means that all the elation, all the intensity in your prayer was not born of God's presence, of your faith in Him, of your longing for Him, of your awareness of Him; it was born of nothing but your concern for him or her or it, not for God. How can we feel surprised, then, that this absence of God affects us? It is we who make ourselves absent, it is we who grow cold the moment we are no longer concerned with God. Why? Because He does not matter so much.

There are other ways too in which God is "absent". As long as we ourselves are real, as long as we are truly ourselves, God can be present and can do something with us. But the moment we try to be what we are not, there is nothing left to say or have; we become a fictitious personality, an unreal presence, and this unreal presence cannot be approached by God.

In order to be able to pray, we must be within the situation which is defined as the kingdom of God. We must recognise that He is God, that He is King, we must surrender to Him. We must at least be concerned with His will, even if we are not yet capable of fulfilling it. But if we are not, if we treat God like the rich young man who could not follow Christ because he was too rich, then how can we meet Him? So often what we would like to have through prayer, through the deep relationship with God which we long for, is simply another period of happiness; we are not prepared to sell all that we have in order to buy the pearl of great price. Then how should we get this pearl of great price? Is that what we expect to get? Is it not the same as in human relationships: when a man or a woman experiences love for another, other people no longer matter in the same way. To put it in a short formula from the ancient world, "When a man has a bride, he is no longer surrounded by men and women, but by people."

Isn't that what could, what should

happen with regard to all our riches when we turn to God? Surely they should become pale and grey, just a general background against which the only figure that matters would appear in intense relief? We would like just one touch of heavenly blue in the general picture of our life, in which there are so many dark sides. God is prepared to be outside it, He is prepared to take it up completely as a cross, but He is not prepared to be simply part of our life.

So when we think of the absence of God, is it not worth while to ask ourselves whom we blame for it? We always blame God, we always accuse Him, either straight to His face or in front of people, of being absent, of never being there when He is needed, never answering when He is addressed. At times we are more "pious" (very much in inverted commas), and we say piously "God is testing my patience, my faith, my humility." We find all sorts of ways of turning God's judgment on us into a new way of praising ourselves. We are so patient that we can put up even with God!

Is this not true? When I was a young priest I preached a sermon, one of the many I preached in a parish, and a young girl

39

came up to me and said "Father Anthony, you must be appallingly evil." I said "I am certainly evil, but how do you know that?" She said "Because you have described our sins so well that you must have committed them all yourself!" Of course, the shocking description of evil thoughts and evil attitudes which I am giving you now are probably mine and not yours, but perhaps they are yours too, however little.

What we must start with, if we wish to pray, is the certainty that we are sinners in need of salvation, that we are cut off from God and that we cannot live without Him and that all we can offer God is our desperate longing to be made such that God will receive us, receive us in repentance, receive us with mercy and with love. And so from the outset prayer is really our humble ascent towards God, a moment when we turn Godwards, shy of coming near, knowing that if we meet Him too soon, before His grace has had time to help us to be capable of meeting Him, it will be judgment. And all we can do is to turn to Him with all the reverence, all the veneration, the worshipful adoration, the fear of God of which we are capable, with all the attention and earnestness which we may possess, and ask Him to do something with us that will make us capable of meeting Him face to face, not for judgment, nor for condemnation, but for eternal life.

I would like to remind you of the parable of the Pharisee and the Publican. The publican comes and stands at the rear of the church. He knows that he stands condemned; he knows that in terms of justice there is no hope for him because he is an outsider to the kingdom of God, the kingdom of righteousness or the kingdom of love, because he belongs neither to the realm of righteousness nor to the realm of love. But in the cruel, the violent, the ugly life he leads, he has learnt something of which the righteous Pharisee has no idea. He has learnt that in a world of competition, in a world of predatory animals, in a world of cruelty and heartlessness, the only hope one can have is an act of mercy, an act of compassion, a completely unexpected act which is rooted neither in duty nor in natural relationships, which will suspend the action of the cruel, violent, heartless world in which we live. All he knows, for instance, from being himself an extortioner, a moneylender, a thief, and so forth, is that there are moments when for no reason, because it is not part of the world's outlook, he will forgive a debt, because suddenly his heart has become mild and vulnerable; that on another occasion he may not get someone put into prison because a face will have reminded him of something or a voice has gone straight to his heart. There is no logic in this. It is not part of the world's outlook nor is it a way in which he normally behaves. It is something that breaks through, which is completely nonsensical, which he cannot resist; and he knows also, probably, how often he himself was saved from final catastrophe by this intrusion of the unexpected and the impossible, mercy, compassion, forgiveness. So he stands at the rear of the church, knowing that all the realm inside the church is a realm of righteousness and divine love to which he does not belong and into which he cannot enter. But he knows from experience also that the impossible does occur and that is why he says "Have mercy, break the laws of righteousness, break the laws of religion, come down in mercy to us who have no right to be either forgiven or allowed in". And I think this is where we should start continuously all over again.

You probably remember the two passages from St. Paul where he says "My power is manifest in weakness". Weakness is not the kind of weakness which we show by sinning and forgetting God, but the kind of weakness which means being completely supple, completely transparent, completely abandoned in the hands of God. We usually try to be strong and we prevent God from manifesting His power.

You remember how you were taught to write when you were small. Your mother put a pencil in your hand, took your hand in hers and began to move it. Since you did not know at all what she meant to do, you left your hand completely free in hers. This is what I mean by the power of God being manifest in weakness. You could think of that also in the terms of a sail. A sail can catch the wind and be used to manoeuvre a boat only because it is so frail. If instead of a sail you put a solid board, it would not work; it is the weakness of the sail that makes it sensitive to the wind. The same is true of the gauntlet and the surgical glove.

43

How strong is the gauntlet, how frail is the glove, yet in intelligent hands it can work miracles because it is so frail. So one of the things which God continues to try to teach us is to replace the imaginary and minute amount of disturbing strength we have by this frailty of surrender, of abandonment in the hands of God. I will give you an example of this.

Twenty-five years ago a friend of mine who had two children was killed during the liberation of Paris. His children had always hated me because they were jealous that their father had a friend, but when the father died they turned to me because I had been their father's friend. One of his children was a girl of fifteen who came to see me one day in my surgery (I was a doctor before I became a priest), and she saw that, apart from my medical paraphernalia, I had a book of the Gospels on my desk. So with all the certainty of youth she said "I can't understand how a man who is supposed to be educated can believe in such stupid things." I said "Have you read it?" She said "No". Then I said "Remember it is only the most stupid people who pass judgments on things they do not know."

After that she read the Gospels and she was so interested that her whole life changed, because she started to pray and God gave her an experience of His presence and she lived by it for a while. Then she fell ill with an incurable disease and she wrote me a letter when I had already become a priest and was in England, and said "Since my body has begun to grow weak and to die out, my spirit has become livelier than ever and I perceive the divine presence so easily and so joyfully." I wrote to her again: "Don't expect it will last. When you have lost a little bit more of your strength, you will no longer be able to turn and cast yourself Godwards and then you will feel that you have no access to God." After a while she wrote again and said "Yes, I have become so weak now that I can't make the effort of moving Godwards or even longing actively and God has gone", but I said "Now do something else. Try to learn humility in the real, deep sense of this word."

The word "humility" comes from the Latin word "*humus*" which means fertile ground. To me, humility is not what we often make of it: the sheepish way of trying to imagine that we are the worst of all and trying to convince others that our artificial ways of behaving show that we are aware of that. Humility is the situation of the earth. The earth is always there, always taken for granted, never remembered, always trodden on by everyone, somewhere we cast and pour out all the refuse, all we don't need. It's there, silent and accepting everything and in a miraculous way making out of all the refuse new richness in spite of corruption, transforming corruption itself into a power of life and a new possibility of creativeness, open to the sunshine, open to the rain, ready to receive any seed we sow and capable of bringing thirtyfold, sixtyfold, a hundredfold out of every seed. I said to this woman "Learn to be like this before God; abandoned, surrendered, ready to receive anything from people and anything from God." Indeed she got a great deal from people; within six months her husband got tired of having a dying wife and 'abandoned her, so refuse was poured generously, but God also shone His light and gave His rain, because after a little while she wrote to me and said "I am completely finished. I can't move Godwards, but it is God who steps down to me."

This is not only a story to illustrate what I said, but something to the point; this is the weakness in which God can manifest His power and this is the situation in which the absence of God can become the presence of God. We cannot capture God. But whenever we stand, either like the Publican or like this girl, outside the realm of "right", only in the realm of mercy, we can meet God.

Try to think about the absence of God, and do realise that before you can knock at the door—and remember that it is not only at the door of the Kingdom understood in the general way, but that Christ really says "I am the door"—before you knock at the door, you must realise that you are outside. If you spend your time imagining that in a mad way you are already in the kingdom of God, there is certainly no point in knocking at any door for it to be opened. Obviously, you must look round trying to see where are the angels and the saints, and where the mansion is which belongs to you, and when you see nothing but darkness or walls, you can quite legitimately find it surprising that Paradise is so unattractive. We must all realise that we are not yet in it, that we are still outsiders to the kingdom of God, and then ask ourselves "Where is the door and how does one knock at it?"

In the next chapter we will try to go deeper into this subject of knocking at the door and the attempt to go inside, to become an inmate of Paradise, of the place where prayer is possible.

KNOCKING AT
THE DOOR

AS I said in speaking of the way in which we perceive the absence of God—which is obviously not objective but subjective—unless we are aware that we are outside the kingdom of God, that we need to knock at a door to be allowed in, we may spend a great deal of our lives in imagining that we are inside, behaving as though we were, and never reaching that depth where the kingdom of God unfolds itself in all its beauty, its truth and its glory.

When I say that we are outsiders, I do not mean simply that there is a situation in which we are radically outside or radically inside. We should think rather in terms of an increasing progression from depth to depth, from height to height, whichever formula you prefer, so that at every step we already possess something which is rich, which is deep, and yet always go on longing for and moving towards something richer and deeper. This is very important to remember, because we are extraordinarily rich, even while we are outside. God gives us so much, we are so rich intellectually and emotionally, our lives are so full, that we may imagine that there can be nothing more than this, that we have found fulfilment and wholeness, that we have reached the end of our search. But we must learn that there is always more. We must rejoice that, poor as we are, we are so rich; yet we must long for the true riches of the Kingdom, being careful not to be beguiled by what we already possess so that we turn away from what is ahead of us.

We must remember that all we possess is a gift. The first Beatitude is one of poverty, and only if we live according to this Beatitude can we enter into the kingdom of God. This Beatitude has two aspects. First, there is the very clear fact that we possess nothing which we can keep, whether we want to or not; it is the discovery that I am nothing and that I have nothing—total, irremediable, hopeless poverty. We exist because we have been willed into existence and brought into existence. We have done nothing for it, it was not an act of our free will. We do not possess life in such a way that it is impossible for anyone to take it away from us, and all that we are and all that we possess is ephemeral in this way. We have a body—it will die. We have a mind—yet it is enough for one minute vessel to burst in a brain for the greatest mind to be suddenly extinguished. We have a heart, sensitive and alive—and yet a moment comes when we would like to pour out all our sympathy, all our understanding for someone who is in need, and at that moment there is nothing but a stone in our breast.

So, in a way, we can say that we possess nothing because we are masters of nothing which is in our possession. And this could lead us, not to the sense of belonging to the kingdom of God and rejoicing in it, but to despair—if we did not remember that although none of these things are ours in such a way that they cannot be taken away from us, yet we *are* in possession of them. This is the second aspect of the Beatitude. We are rich, and everything which we possess is a gift and a sign of the love of God and the love of men, it is a continuous gift of divine love; and as long as we possess nothing, love divine is manifested continuously and fully. But everything we take into our own hands to possess is taken out of the realm of love. Certainly it becomes ours, but love is lost. And it is only those who give everything away who become aware of true, total, final, irremediable, spiritual poverty, and who possess the love of God expressed in all His gifts. One of our theologians has said "All the food of this world is divine love made edible." I think this is true and the moment we try to be rich by keeping something safely in our hands, we are the losers, because as long as we have nothing in our hands, we can take, leave, do whatever we want.

This is the Kingdom, the sense that we are free from possession, and this freedom establishes us in a relationship where everything is love—human love and love divine.

Now if we reason in these terms, we can transfer the same idea to what was said earlier. Yes, we are rich. Yet we should never be beguiled by what we possess into imagining that now we can demolish the old barns and build new ones in order to store more of our riches. Nothing can be stored—nothing except the kingdom of God itself. And so we can discard one thing after another in order to go ahead free—free of being rich. Have you never noticed that to be rich always means an impoverishment on another level? It is enough for you to say "I have this watch, it is mine", and close your hand on it, to be in possession of a watch and to have lost a hand. And if you close your mind on your riches, if you close your heart so that you can keep what is in it safe, never to lose it, then it becomes as small as the thing on which you have closed yourself in.

Now if that is true, the moment you reach rock bottom, the moment you are aware of your utter dispossession of all things, then you are on the fringe of the kingdom of God, you are nearly aware that God is love and that He is upholding you by His love. And at that point you can say two things simultaneously. You can pray out of your utter misery, dereliction and poverty, and you can rejoice that you are so rich with the love of God. But this is only if you have come to the point of discovering it, because as long as you imagine you are rich there is nothing to thank God for, and you cannot be aware of being loved. Too often the kind of thanksgiving we offer is too much a general thanksgiving, and the kind of repentance we bring to God is too much a general repentance.

I have experienced this once, in a most unromantic and unspiritual way. When I was a teenager I remember going to a place, and I calculated my journey very well because I hoped I would arrive at the moment when people have lunch, and I thought that if I arrived in time they couldn't possibly make me wait in the next room without giving me something to eat. But, of course, my train was late and I arrived after lunch, ravenously hungry. I was with a friend, and since we were really too hungry to go on we asked whether there was anything they could give us. They said "We have half a cucumber." We looked at this cucumber and at each other and thought "Is that all God can give us?" Then my friend said "And now, let us say grace." I thought "Goodness for a cucumber!" My friend was a better believer than I and more pious, so we read None together, and then we read a few more prayers, then we read the blessing of the food, and all the time I had difficulty in detaching myself from the half cucumber, of which a quarter would be mine, and then we broke the cucumber and ate it. In all my life I haven't been so grateful to God for any amount or quantity of food. I ate it as one would eat sacred food. I ate it carefully, not to miss any moment of this rich delight of the fresh cucumber, and after we had finished I had no hesitation in saying, "And now, let us give thanks to the Lord", and we started again in gratitude.

We cannot live a life of prayer, we cannot go ahead Godwards, unless we are free from possession in order to have two hands to offer and a heart absolutely open—not like a purse which we are afraid of keeping open because our money will drop out of it, but like an open and empty purse—and an intelligence completely open to the unknown and the unexpected. This is the way in which we are rich and yet totally free from richness. And this is the point at which we can speak of being outside the Kingdom and yet be so rich inside and yet also so free.

This is true, for instance, when we fast.

I don't mean the fasting and abstinence that affects only the stomach but that attitude of sobriety which allows you, or compels you, never to get enslaved by anything. This is a question of our whole conduct of life. First of all it affects our imagination because that is a point at which sin begins. One of our Orthodox writers, in the ninth century, said that the sins of the flesh are the sins which the spirit commits against the flesh. It is not the flesh that is responsible, and I think in that sense we must learn to control our imagination. As long as our imagination has not taken hold of us, things are outside us; once our imagination has got entangled and imprisoned in things, then we are glued to things. You know there are such things as meat and vegetables and puddings and so on. As an objective fact you know it. If you settle down and ask yourself "I'm not really hungry but there are so many nice things one can eat, what would I fancy?" In five minutes' time you will have projected tentacles over a variety of things. You will be like Gulliver, knit to the ground by one hair and another hair and another hair; each of the hairs is really nothing, but the sum total will keep you solidly tied down. Once you have allowed your imagination full sway, things are much more difficult. In that respect we must be sober and we must fight for freedom. There is a great deal of difference between attachment and love, between hunger and greed, between a live interest and curiosity, and so forth. Every one of our natural propensities has got a counterpart which is marked by evil and which is one of the ways in which we get enslaved. This is what I meant by withdrawing tentacles. To begin with, say "no". If you haven't said "no" in time, you are in for a fight. But then be ruthless about it, because reason and detachment are more precious than what you get as a slave in terms of enjoyment.

Now if what I have said so far is true, we must knock at a door. At this point certain problems become very acute. If the door was that of some church, it would be very simple, we would come and knock. But the trouble is that we usually do not know where to knock. How often people want to pray and they ask themselves "Now where is the focus of this prayer? Where should I turn my gaze and my heart?" If you are a Moslem, it is simple. You turn towards Mecca. But even so, once we have turned eastwards, what then? You cannot focus on things which are less than God. The moment you try to focus on an imaginary god, or a god you can imagine, you are in great danger of placing an idol between yourself and the real God. This is a thought which was expressed as early as the fourth century by St. Gregory of Nazianzus. He said that the moment we put a visible sign in front of ourselves, whether it be a crucifix, a tabernacle, an icon or an invisible image—God as we imagine Him, or Christ as we have seen Him in paintings—and we focus our attention on that, then we have placed a barrier between ourselves and God, because we take the image which we have formed for the person to whom we address our prayer. What we must do is to collect all the knowledge of God which we possess in order to come into His presence, but then remember that all we know about God is our past, as it were, behind our back, and we are standing face to face with God in all His complexity, all His simplicity, so close and yet unknown. Only if we stand completely open before the unknown, can the unknown reveal itself, Himself, as He chooses to reveal Himself to us as we are today. So, with this open-heartedness and open-mindedness, we must stand before God without trying to give Him a shape or to imprison Him in concepts and images, and we must knock at a door.

Where? The Gospel tells us that the kingdom of God is within us first of all. If we cannot find the kingdom of God within us, if we cannot meet God within, in the very depth of ourselves, our chances of meeting Him outside ourselves are very remote. When Gagarin came back from space and made his remarkable statement that he never saw God in Heaven, one of our priests in Moscow remarked "If you have not seen Him on earth, you will never see Him in Heaven." This is also true of what I am speaking about. If we cannot find a contact with God under our own skin, as it were, in this very small world which I am, then the chances are very slight that even if I meet Him face to face, I will recognise Him. St. John Chrysostom said "Find the door of your heart, you will discover it is the door of the kingdom of God." So it is inward that we must turn, and not outward—but inward in a very special way. I am not saying that we must become introspective. I don't mean that we must go inward in the way one does in psychoanalysis or psychology. It is not a journey into my *own* inwardness, it is a journey *through* my own self, in order to emerge from the deepest level of self into the place where He is, the point at which God and I meet.

So this question of incipient prayer has, therefore, two aspects: first, this going inwards, and secondly, the use of words in prayer and the direction in which to turn them.

I will speak now of the second point. Towards what, towards whom shall I turn the sharp edge of my prayer? Very often people try to shout into the sky and they are surprised to discover that the sky is empty and does not echo back. It is not there that one can find an echo. A spiritual writer of the seventh century, St. John Climacus, has written that a prayer, words of prayer, are like an arrow. But to possess an arrow is not enough. If you want to hit a target, you must have a bow with a good string, and a good arm to pull. If you have a good bow and cannot pull, your arrow will just fly a few yards and fall short. If you do not shoot your shaft with a powerful arm, it will not hit the target. What we need is the bow, the string and the arm, and the strength. Now, given that the words of prayer are the shaft, we are aiming at the deepest point where God is to be found within us; we must turn our bow inwards to hit ourselves at that deepest point. Secondly, we must provide the arrow with all the conditions that will allow it to fly forcefully. Very often we are inattentive in prayer, our heart is not in it, and our prayer is not upheld by our life. Here, if you wish, are analogies with the bow, the string and the strength.

There are moments when one can make attempts at breaking through into the depths by calling to Him who is at the root and depth of all things, but you will see perfectly well where you are going and where to aim the prayer: not back, not upwards, but deeper, deeper—at every resistance there is in the way, at every covering fallacy, at everything that prevents you from piercing through into that very depth. And so prayer will become something perfectly feasible, although a hard, arduous, daring exercise.

First of all, then, we must choose a prayer. That is very important. Just as it is important to use the right words if you are in a relationship with someone, so it is with a prayer. Whichever one we choose, it must be a prayer that makes sense to us and a prayer which does not make us uneasy. I must admit that the perusal of manuals of prayer very often leaves me very uneasy. I feel that if God was really present, concretely there in front of me, I would certainly not dare to make all these flat discourses to Him and tell Him things about Himself that He has known long before I ever came into the world. So there is a need for choice, because if you are ashamed of your prayer, God may be uneasy about you and the prayer too, and you will never be able to bring it to God wholeheartedly. The first thing, then, is really to find words of prayer that are worthy of you and worthy of God. I say "worthy of you and worthy of God" because if they are good enough for you, then God can accept them, but if they are not good enough for you, leave God alone. He has heard better things than that. Yet we must not try to find extraordinary words; one of the dangers in prayer is to try to find words that will be somehow on the level of God. Unfortunately, as none of us are on a level with God, we fall short and waste a great deal of time in trying to find the right words.

Without attempting to cover all the ground, I would just like to give you an image of the worthiness of an act of worship or words of worship. In the life of Moses, in Hebrew folklore, there is a remarkable passage. Moses finds a shepherd in the desert. He spends the day with the shepherd and helps him milk his ewes, and at the end of the day he sees that the shepherd puts the best milk he has in a wooden bowl, which he places on a flat stone some distance away. So Moses asks him what it is for, and the shepherd replies "This is God's milk." Moses is puzzled and asks him what he means. The shepherd says "I always take the best milk I possess, and I bring it as an offering to God." Moses, who is far more sophisticated than the shepherd with his naïve faith, asks, "And does God drink it?" "Yes," replies the shepherd, "He does." Then Moses feels compelled to enlighten the poor shepherd and he explains that God, being pure spirit, does not drink milk. Yet the shepherd is sure that He does, and so they have a short argument, which ends with Moses telling the shepherd to hide behind the bushes to find out whether in fact God does come to drink the milk. Moses then goes out to pray in the desert. The shepherd hides, the night comes, and in the moonlight the shepherd sees a little fox that comes trotting from the desert, looks right, looks left and heads straight towards the milk, which he laps up, and disappears into the desert again. The next morning Moses finds the shepherd quite depressed and downcast. "What's the matter?" he asks. The shepherd says "You were right, God is pure spirit and He doesn't want my milk." Moses is surprised. He says "You should be happy. You know more about God than you did before." "Yes, I do" says the shepherd, "but the only thing I could do to express my love for Him has been taken away from me." Moses sees the point. He retires into the desert and prays hard. In the night in a vision, God speaks to him and says "Moses, you were wrong. It is true that I am pure spirit. Nevertheless I always accepted with gratitude the milk which the shepherd offered me, as the expression of his love, but since, being pure spirit, I do not need the milk, I shared it with this little fox, who is very fond of milk."

I have tried to point out, first of all, that your prayer must be turned inwards, not towards a God of Heaven nor towards a God far off, but towards God who is closer to you than you are aware; and secondly, that the first act of prayer is to choose such words of prayer as are completely true to what you are, words which you are not ashamed of, which express you adequately and are worthy of you—and then offer them to God with all the intelligence of which you are capable. You must also put all the heart you can into an act of worship, an act of recognition of God, an act of cherishing, which is the true meaning of charity, an action which involves you in the mind, in the heart, and an action which is completely adequate to what you are.

The first thing which I suggest, therefore, is that you should ask yourself what words of prayer make sense for you to offer to God, whether they be your own or those of other people. Ask yourself also how much they touch your heart, to what extent you are capable of concentrating your mind on them—for if you cannot be attentive to the words you say, why should God? How can He receive them as an expression of love if you do not put your heart into them, if you have only put in a certain amount of courtesy together with a certain amount of absent-mindedness?

And then if you learn to use a prayer you have chosen at moments when you can give all your attention to the divine presence and offer God this prayer, gradually what happens is that the awareness of God grows within you to such an extent that whether you are with people, listening, speaking or whether you are alone working, this awareness is so strong that even if you are with people you will still be able to pray. The analogy which some of our spiritual writers give works on two different levels: one is simpler and cruder and, I think, expresses very well what they are trying to say, the other is loftier.

The simpler and cruder one is something which one of our great spiritual guides, Theophan the Recluse, says: "The awareness of God shall be with you as clearly as a toothache." When you have a toothache, you don't forget it at all. You may be talking, you may be reading, you may be scrubbing, you may be singing, you may be doing anything; the toothache is there continuously present and you cannot escape the ache of its presence. He says in the same way we should develop an ache in our hearts. I don't mean the physical heart, but at the core of us, an ache that will be a desperate longing for God, a feeling that "I am alone, where is He?" at the moment when you have lost touch in prayer.

The loftier way of putting it, of course, is to say that when a great joy has come upon us or a great pain or a great sorrow, we do not forget it in the course of the day. We listen to people, we do our work, we read, we do what we are supposed to, and the pain of bereavement, the awareness of joy, of the exhilarating news is with us incessantly. This should also be the sense of the presence of God. And if the sense of the presence of God is as clear as that, then one can pray while one does other things. One can pray while one works physically, but one can also pray when one is with people, listening or being engaged in some sort of conversation or relationship. But, as I said, this is not the first thing that happens to us, and I think we must school ourselves to an attitude of worshipful attention and of broken-heartedness first, in those conditions which allow it, because it is so easy to get inattentive, to slip from alertness to dreaming in prayer. Let us start to learn this sort of prayerful attention, of complete stability, of worshipful adoration, and of surrender to God at moments when we can do it with an undivided mind and heart, and then one can make attempts in other situations.

We will go on with this subject in the next chapter by showing the way one can take one or two prayers and use them to break through into our own depth, towards the place where God is. In addition to that, I will try to explain how one can go inward, for this is another exercise. Do not forget the little fox, he can be most useful for your life of prayer. And while we are on the subject of foxes, if you want to learn how one makes friends with God, learn from another fox in the book by Saint-Exupéry called *The Little Prince* about how one makes friends with one who is extremely sensitive, vulnerable and shy.

GOING INWARD

I HAVE said that one of the problems which we must all face and solve is: where should I direct my prayer? The answer I have suggested is that we should direct it at ourselves. Unless the prayer which you intend to offer to God is important and meaningful to you first, you will not be able to present it to the Lord. If you are inattentive to the words you pronounce, if your heart does not respond to them, or if your life is not turned in the same direction as your prayer, it will not reach out Godwards. So the first thing is, as I said, to choose a prayer which you can say with all your mind, with all your heart and with all your will—a prayer which does not necessarily have to be a great example of liturgical art, but which must be true, something which should not fall short of what you want to express. You must understand this prayer, with all the richness and precision it possesses.

In the use of words there are three things

we can do. We can use spontaneous prayer, the kind of prayer that gushes out of our own souls; we can use short vocal prayers which are very short, extremely intense in their content and wide so that they can contain as many meanings as possible; and we can use what one calls, at times in a rather unpleasant way, ready-made prayers, which range from the flattest productions of people who are trying to invent prayers for all occasions, to the expressions of the saints' deepest experience, expressed in the prayers that they did not invent but which the Holy Spirit coined within their lives and within their hearts. I would like to say something about each of these categories.

Spontaneous prayer is possible in two situations: either at moments when we have become vividly aware of God, when this awareness calls out of us a response of worship, of joy, all the forms of response which we are capable of giving, being ourselves and facing the living God, or when we become aware suddenly of the deathly danger in which we are when we come to God, moments when we suddenly shout out from the depths of despair and dereliction, and also from the sense that there is no hope of salvation for us unless God saves us.

These two situations are the two extreme poles—the vision of ourselves in the desperate situation in which we are, Godless, lonely, longing, and yet incapable of breaking through; or the marvel of suddenly finding ourselves face to face with God when we can pray spontaneously and it doesn't matter much what words we use. We can go on repeating "my joy, my joy". We can say words because the words do not matter, the words are merely a way of sustaining a mood, of speaking foolishly, madly of our love or of our despair. You remember the passage in the Gospel concerning the Transfiguration in which Peter says to Christ "Shall we make three tents for you, for Moses and for Elijah?" The Gospel says he was speaking nonsense because he was out of himself. He was faced with something so overwhelming that he said whatever came into his mind, he blundered out something that expressed his feelings.

Now, if we imagine that we can sustain spontaneous prayer throughout our life, we are in a childish delusion. Spontaneous prayer must gush out of our souls, we cannot simply turn on a tap and get it out. It is not there for us to draw from to use at any moment. It comes from the depths of our soul, from either wonder or distress, but it does not come from the middle situation in which we are neither overwhelmed by the divine presence nor overwhelmed by a sense of who we are and the position in which we are. So that, at those moments, to try to use a spontaneous prayer is a completely illusory exercise. There are whole periods when you are neither at the bottom of the sea nor at the top of the peak, when you have got to do something about praying, and that is the period when you cannot pray from spontaneity but you can pray from conviction. This is very important, because many people who begin a life of prayer think that unless they feel very strongly about the words and phrases they use, they are not being sincere. This is not true. One can at times be perfectly sincere in the lucidity of one's mind, in the straightness of one's will, although at a given moment these words, or it can be gestures, do not express what I feel now.

The example that comes to me is this. When you live in your family, and you work out of doors and are doing a heavy kind of work, you may come back physically worn out. If at that moment your mother, your sister, your father or whoever else, said "Do you love me?" you would say "I do." If the other person goes on investigating, "Do you really love me at this moment?" what you could honestly have said is "No, I feel nothing but my aching back and worn out body." But you are perfectly right in saying "I love you" because you know that underneath all the exhaustion, there is a live current of love. And when Christ says "those who love me will keep my commandments" He does not say that "if you love me you will go from one emotion into another, one state of rapture into another, one theological vision to another", He just says "If you believe my words then live up to what you have received", and "live up" means always live a little bit above one's means, as it were. To do more than you could have done spontaneously.

So there is a need for some sort of prayer which is not spontaneous but which is truly rooted in conviction. To find this you can draw from a great many of the existing prayers. We already have a rich panoply of prayers which were wrought in the throes of faith, by the Holy Spirit. For example, we have the psalms, we have so many short and long prayers in the liturgical wealth of all the Churches from which we can draw. What matters is that you should learn and know enough of such prayers so that at the right moment you are able to find the right prayers. It is a question of learning by heart enough meaningful passages, from the psalms or from the prayers of the saints. Each of us is sensitive to certain particular passages. Mark these passages that go deep into your heart, that move you deeply, that make sense, that express something which is already within your experience, either of sin, or of bliss in God, or of struggle. Learn those passages, because one day when you are so completely low, so profoundly desperate that you cannot call out of your soul any spontaneous expression, any spontaneous wording, you will discover that these words come up and offer themselves to you as a gift of God, as a gift of the Church, as a gift of holiness, helping our simple lack of strength. And then you really need the prayers you have learnt and made a part of yourself.

In the Orthodox Church, we have morning and evening prayers, which are, on the whole, longer than the ones commonly used in the West. It should take about half an hour in the morning, half an hour in the evening, to read these prayers. A person will try to learn them by heart so that at other moments he or she can draw from them. But it is not enough just to learn prayers by heart. A prayer makes sense only if it is lived. Unless they are "lived", unless life and prayer become completely interwoven, prayers become a sort of polite madrigal which you offer to God at moments when you are giving time to Him.

If in your morning prayers you have said a phrase, you must live up to this phrase in the course of the day. And I think that, apart from learning as many meaningful passages as you can, you must make a rule that when you have discovered one phrase which makes sense to you—in the reading of the Gospel, in the reading of the New or Old Testament in general, in praying with words from the liturgy—you must try to apply it in the course of the day ruthlessly, for as long as you can. You may imagine that you are capable of taking up a phrase like this and living it throughout the course of a whole day. But it is extremely difficult. If you can keep to one sentence of one prayer for an hour without breaking the rule you will be lucky, but do it! Say, "I have read this prayer, my heart is ready, O Lord, my heart is ready, for half an hour I will make sure that my heart is open to God and ready to obey His will." Half an hour, not more, then give yourself a respite and turn to something else because, if you try to keep to one sentence which is absolute and difficult, in the end you will simply say to yourself "Can't do it any more" and you will end up doing nothing. But if you say "I have three or four or five sentences as slogans for the day and I will try to apply this from the moment I have read it until 10 o'clock in the morning, then I'll move to the next one, then to the next one", you will see that gradually all the words of prayer, all the thoughts and feelings the saints express in their prayers come alive in you, they begin to go deep into your will and to mould your will and your body, because it is with your body that you have to apply commandments.

However, you may say "I don't feel very strongly about these words." If these words express a basic conviction but you feel nothing at the moment, turn to God in repentance and say to God "This is my basic Christian faith, and look, I don't feel anything about it", and then from that point you may discover that you suddenly burst into spontaneous prayer. You can express to God your sorrow, your misery, your disgust with yourself, and you come back with the determined will to tell God what is true and that your will is united with His will.

A last way in which we can pray is the use, more or less continuous, of a vocal prayer that serves as a background, a walking stick, throughout the day and throughout life. What I have in mind now is something which is specifically used by the Orthodox. It is what we call the "Jesus prayer", a prayer which is centred on the name of Jesus. "Lord Jesus Christ, son of God, have mercy on me a sinner." This prayer is used by monks and nuns but also it is used by our lay people. It is the prayer of stability, because it is the prayer that is not discursive—we do not move from one thought to the other—it is a prayer that places us face to face with God through a profession of faith concerning Him, and it defines a situation concerning us. It is the profession of faith which, according to the mind of most Orthodox ascetics and mystics, is a summing up of the whole Gospel. We profess the Lordship of Christ, His sovereign right upon us, the fact that He is our Lord and Our God, and this implies that all our life is within His will and that we commit ourselves to His will and to no other way. That is the name of "Jesus" in which we confess the reality of the Incarnation and all that the Incarnation stands for. Christ in whom we see the Incarnate Word of God in the line of the Old and the New Testament, the anointed of Yahweh. Then the perfect profession of faith, of what He is—the Son of God. This is not only a profession of faith in Jesus Christ, but it also opens up the Trinitarian way because He is the Son of the Father and no one can recognise in the prophet of Galilee the Incarnate Son of God unless the

Holy Spirit teaches him to see, to understand and to commit himself. So here we have the fourth profession of faith that allows us to stand face to face with God in truth, and profess in spirit. And then, "have mercy on us." "Have mercy" is the English rendering of the word "eleison". When you say the Kyrie Eleison, you are using Greek words which mean "Lord, have mercy."

Why I want to insist on these words which we use in prayer is that in all modern languages words have specialised and narrowed meanings as contrasted with ancient languages. Very often we use words of prayer which are extremely rich but we do not notice the depth of what we say, because we take the words for what they mean in our ordinary speech, while they could have deep echoes in our hearts if we only connected them with other things we know.

I would like to give you an example of this which may shock classical scholars because the philology implied is doubtful, but since it is based on a pun made centuries ago by the Greek Spiritual

Fathers, who knew their language and were not shy of making a pun, I will take advantage of it too. Most of us use the words "Kyrie eleison", or "Lord, have mercy", at some moments of our lives. We are at least aware that they exist, and know approximately what we mean by them. On the whole, it is an appeal to God for mercy, for compassion, for warmth of heart. Now the point at which the classical student may find fault with me and with the Greek Fathers is that some of them derive "eleison" from the same root as the Greek words "olive tree", "olive", "olive oil". However, let us leave the argument to scholars and have a look at what could be conveyed to us from the point of view of the Scriptures. When we say "Kyrie eleison", we may be content with the sense that it is a general appeal to God's mercy. In this case it will not satisfy us, because we cannot put the whole of our life into this "Lord, have mercy", and besides, the words themselves do not mean much in our ordinary speech. But if you think of the olive tree, of the olive in the Old and New Testaments, you will see the following: the first time the olive and the twig of the olive tree appear is at the end of the Flood, when the twig is brought to Noah by a dove. (Is it the same dove that hovered over Christ on the day of His baptism?) This olive twig means that the wrath of God has come to an end, that forgiveness is freely given, that time and new possibilities open up ahead of us. This is the first situation. However, we cannot always follow this way, because it is not enough just to have time and new possibilities opening up if we are sick at heart, if we are broken in will or if we are incapable in mind or body either of discerning or of following the path. We need healing, so remember the oil which the Good Samaritan poured on the wounds of the man who had fallen victim to the robbers. The healing power of God will make it possible for us to take advantage of the cessation of His wrath, of the gift of forgiveness that is offered and, indeed, of the gift of time and space and eternity.

Another image is that of the anointing of priests and kings, who among the people of Israel were called upon to stand on a threshold between the world divine and the human world, between the unity and harmony of the will of God and the diversity and complexities—not to speak of the tensions and oppositions—of the human world. To be able to stand there, a man needs more than human capability; he needs a divine gift. This was signified at the anointing given to both priests and kings. But in the New Testament all of us are priests and kings, and our vocation as human beings and as Christians is beyond what a human being could achieve. We are called upon to become and to be living members of the Body of Christ, temples on a soil pure and worthy of the Holy Spirit, and partakers of the divine nature. All this is beyond our own human capabilities, and yet we need to be human to the full, in the profound way in which a Christian thinks of humanity in the image of the Incarnate Son of God. To do this we need the grace and the help of God. All this is shown us in the same image.

Now, if we reflected with the same simplicity—it takes only a dictionary and a Bible and some thinking—and if we thought as simply and as directly about the other words we use in prayer, then they would grow remarkably rich intellectually. Then we could pay more attention to what we say, and our prayer would not just be one of empty words or words which are merely the symbol of something from which the true meaning is lost. Then before we said "Kyrie eleison"—"Lord, have mercy on me; Lord, show me compassion; Lord, pour out Thy love and tenderness on me"—we should have thought about the situation we are in. Have we fallen to our lowest depth? Are we faced with infinite possibilities, and at the same time unable to realise any of them because we are so deeply wounded? Are we healed, and yet confronted with a vocation so great that it humbles us to think of it because it is beyond us? Yet it can be fulfilled only if God grants us the power to do so. This implies an attentive perusal of words. It also implies such a treatment of words as to make them part of our emotions and that we bring and collect around them all the intensity and depth of our personal life. But if the words we use are not made real by the way we live, they will still be meaning-less and lead nowhere, because they will be like a bow that we cannot shoot for lack of a string. It is absolutely pointless to ask God for something which we ourselves are not prepared to do. If we say "O God, make me free from this or that temptation" while at the same time seeking every possible way of falling to just such a temptation, hoping now that God is in control, that He will get us out of it, then we do not stand much chance. God gives us strength but we must use it. When, in our prayers, we ask God to give us strength to do something in His Name, we are *not* asking Him to do it *instead* of us because we are too feeble to be willing to do it for ourselves.

The lives of the saints are enlightening in this respect, and in the life of St. Philip Neri just such an occasion is described. He was an irascible man who quarrelled easily and had violent outbursts of anger and of course endured violent outbursts from his brothers. One day he felt that it could not go on. Whether it was virtue or whether he could no longer endure his brothers his *Vita* does not tell us. The fact is that he ran to the chapel, fell down before a statue of Christ and begged Him to free him of his anger. He then walked out full of hope. The first person he met was one of the brothers who had never aroused the slightest anger in him, but for the first time

85

in his life this brother was offensive and unpleasant to him. So Philip burst out with anger and went on, full of rage, to meet another of his brothers, who had always been a source of consolation and happiness to him. Yet even this man answered him gruffly. So Philip ran back to the chapel, cast himself before the statue of Christ and said "O Lord, have I not asked you to free me from this anger?" And the Lord answered "Yes, Philip, and for this reason I am multiplying the occasions for you to learn."

I think it is very important for us to realise that God will act in this way. He is not going to be crucified for you every day. There is a moment when you must take up your own cross. We must each take up our own cross, and when we ask something in our prayers, we undertake by implication to do it with all our strength, all our intelligence and all the enthusiasm we can put into our actions, and with all the courage and energy we have. In addition, we do it with all the power which God will give us. If we do not do this, we are wasting our time praying. This implies that "Kyrie eleison", or any similar words which we may utter, must be turned against ourselves. Our mind must be formed, moulded to the words, filled and harmonised with them. Our heart must accept them with complete conviction and express them with all the strength of which we are capable, and our will must take hold of them and transform them into action. Therefore, prayer and action should become two expressions of the same situation vis-à-vis God and ourselves and everything around us. Short of that, we are wasting our time. What is the point of telling God about things, and when He gives us strength to combat them, sitting back to wait until He does it for us? What point is there in repeating words which have grown so thin, so meaningless, that they just allow us to keep a cobweb, as it were, between ourselves and God?

Therefore, choose the right words, choose them and fasten all your attention to them, because they are words of truth and the words that God will hear because they are true. Put all your heart into them. Make these words so live with intellectual consciousness because they are true, and make them pierce through to the very depths of your own heart.

Words of prayer have the quality of always being words of commitment. You cannot simply say words of prayer without implying "If I say that, then that is what I am going to do when the occasion lends itself." When you say to God "At all costs, at all costs, O Lord, save me", you must remember that you must put all your will into that, because one day God will say "Here is the price to pay." The ancient writers said "Give your blood and God will give you the Spirit." That is the price. Abandon all, you will receive heaven; abandon enslavement, you will acquire freedom. As your will is already engaged not only in the act of praying but in all the consequences of this prayer, so also must your body be, because a human being is not simply a soul engaged for a while in a body. It is a being which is body and soul, one unique being which is Man.

There is a physical effort to be made in prayer, the physical attention, the physical way in which you pray. Fasting, if food has made you too heavy for prayer, is involved in it too. If you do this, you will be knocking at a door.

Now if we want to go inwards with all these words, to bore down deeper and deeper, the way one bores to get something from the depths of the earth, then we must take a risk, and this risk is that it is very difficult to go inwards. It sounds simple. We all assume that we are deep and that the deeper we go, the more delightful it will be. It is not quite as simple as that. True, when we have come to a certain depth it is all right, but on the way it looks very much like the stories of the quest of the Grail. There are all sorts of monsters to be met with on the way, and the monsters are not devils, they are not our neighbour, they are just ourselves. This makes it more distasteful and much more difficult to do.

Generally, it is greed, fear and curiosity which make us live outwardly. A French scientist who worked in America, Alexis Carrel, said in a book called *Man the Unknown* that if you ask yourself where your personality ends you will see that the tongue of a greedy person is projected like tentacles towards all the edibles of the world; the eyes of the curious person are like tentacles projected and attached to everything around; the ears of the eavesdropper become long and wide and go far far afield. If you could draw a picture of what you look like in those terms, you would see that precious little is left of you inside, because everything is extroverted. So that the first thing one must do is to detach the tentacles and bring them in. You cannot go inwards if you are completely outward.

Try an experiment and you will see, you will discover a number of other useful things on the way. Try to find time to stay alone with yourself: shut the door and settle down in your room at a moment when you have nothing else to do. Say "I am now with myself", and just sit with yourself. After an amazingly short time you will most likely feel bored. This teaches us one very useful thing. It gives us insight into the fact that if after ten minutes of being alone with ourselves we feel like that, it is no wonder that others should feel equally bored! Why is this so? It is so because we have so little to offer to our own selves as food for thought, for emotion and for life. If you watch your life carefully you will discover quite soon that we hardly ever live from within outwards; instead we respond to incitement, to excitement. In other words, we live by reflection, by reaction. Something happens and we respond, someone speaks and we answer. But when we are left without anything that stimulates us to think, speak or act, we realise that there is very little in us that will prompt us to action in any direction at all. This is really a very dramatic discovery. We are completely empty, we do not act from within ourselves but accept as our life a life which is actually fed in from outside; we are used to things happening which compel us to do other things. How seldom can we live simply by means of the depth and the richness we assume that there is within ourselves.

There is a passage in Dickens' *Pickwick Papers* which is a very good description of my life and probably also of your lives. Pickwick goes to the club. He hires a cab and on the way he asks innumerable questions. Among the questions, he says "Tell me, how is it possible that such a mean and miserable horse can drive such a big and heavy cab?" The cabbie replies "It's not a question of the horse, Sir, it's a question of the wheels", and Mr. Pickwick says "What do you mean?" The cabbie answers "You see, we have a magnificent pair of wheels which are so well oiled that it is enough for the horse to stir a little for the wheels to begin to turn and then the poor horse must run for its life." Take the way in which we live most of time. We are not the horse that pulls, we are the horse that runs away from the cab in fear of its life.

Because we don't know yet how to act without an outer reason, we discover that we don't know what to do with ourselves, and then we begin to be increasingly bored. So first of all, you must learn to sit with yourself and to face boredom, drawing all the possible conclusions.

After a while this becomes worse than boredom, because we are not simply bored in a way that allows us to say "I am an active person and am of use to my neighbour. I always do good, and for me to be in the state of suspense where I am not doing anything for anyone else is a severe trial." We begin to discover something else. We are bored when we try to get out of this boredom by turning inward to see if there is anything in ourselves that will put an end to it. Quite soon we discover that there is nothing, since all we have to think about we have already thought about dozens of times. All the range of emotions which we have in store are there like a piano which we have closed because we are not used to the piano playing itself. We must have someone else playing on the keys. We are not in the habit of doing nothing, and so it becomes worrying and can lead us to the point of anguish. If you read the Desert Fathers, who had good experience of this, or the monks who spent their lives in monasteries, you will see that there are moments when they simply ran out of their cells shouting for help, trying to meet something or someone, whatever they could find. The devil himself would have been better than this emptiness of self-contemplation. One of the spiritual writers, Theophan the Recluse, says "Most people are like a shaving of wood which is curled round its central emptiness." If we are really honest, we must admit that this is a very apt description of the state of practically all of us.

Then we must be able to fight this

anguish and to say "No, I will stick it through, and I will come to the point where the anguish itself will prompt me to do what good will is incapable of doing." Indeed, a moment comes, a moment of despair and anguish and terror, which makes us turn even deeper inward and cry "Lord, have mercy! I am perishing. Lord, save me!" We discover that there is nothing in us that can give life, or rather is life; that all we called life, imagined life to be, was outside and inside there was nothing.

Then we look into the abyss of nonentity and we feel that the deeper we go into it the less there will be left of us. This is a dangerous moment, this is the moment when we must hesitate.

At this point we have reached the first layer of depth where we begin to be able to knock at a door. For on the layer where we were just resting from our neighbour before we felt bored, on the layer where we are simply bored and feel offended that we should be, on the layer on which we begin to fidget and worry, then feel slightly anguished, we have as yet no reason to cry and shout with a despair that fills all our mind, all our heart, all our will and all our body with a sense that unless God comes I am lost, there is no hope, because I know that if I emerge out of this depth I will simply be back in the realm of delusion, of reflected life, but not real life.

This is the point at which we can begin to knock at a door which is still closed, but beyond which there is hope, that hope which Bartimaeus, the blind man at the gates of Jericho, felt, out of his utmost despair, when Christ was passing.

We know from the Gospels that Bartimaeus found himself landed by the side of the road, hopelessly blind, having lost all faith and all hope in human help, and reduced to beg for his living, to hope not really on charity (the word meaning "cherishing"), but on the kind of charity which consists in throwing coins to someone without ever having seen him. And one day this man, who had now given up hope, who was installed in the dust in his present blindness, heard about the man, a new prophet, who was now working miracles throughout the Holy Land. Had he had eyes he would probably have got up and run throughout the country to find him, but he couldn't possibly keep pace with this itinerant wondermaker. And so he stayed where he was, and the presence of one who might possibly have cured him must have made his despair even greater, even more poignant. And one day he heard a crowd that passed by, a crowd which did not sound like any other crowd. Probably, as the blind do, he had developed the sense of hearing and a sensitiveness greater than ours, because he asked "Who is it that passes by?" and he was told "Jesus of Nazareth". And then he stood at the point of utmost despair and of utmost hope. Utmost hope because Christ was passing within reach, but at the background the looming despair because a few paces would have brought Him level with Bartimaeus, a few more paces and He had gone and would probably never pass by him again. And out of this desperate hope he began to cry and shout "Jesus, son of David, have mercy on me." It was a perfect profession of faith. And at that moment it was because his despair was so deep that he could summon such daring hope in order to be healed, saved, made whole. And Christ heard him.

There is a degree of despair that is linked with total, perfect hope. This is the point at which, having gone inward, we will be able to pray; and then "Lord, have mercy" is quite enough. We do not need to make any of the elaborate discourses we find in manuals of prayer. It is enough simply to shout out of despair "Help!" and you will be heard.

Very often we do not find sufficient intensity in our prayer, sufficient conviction, sufficient faith, because our despair is not deep enough. We want God in addition to so many other things we have, we want His help, but simultaneously we are trying to get help wherever we can, and we keep God in store for our last push. We address ourselves to the princes and the sons of men, and we say "O God, give them strength to do it for me." Very seldom do we turn away from the princes and sons of men and say "I will not ask anyone for help, I would rather have Your help". If our despair comes from sufficient depth, if what we ask for, cry for, is so essential that it sums up all the needs of our life, then we find words of prayer and we will be able to reach the core of the prayer, the meeting with God.

And now, more about turmoil. The link

here is also Bartimaeus. He cried, but what does the Gospel say of everyone around? They tried to silence him, and we can see all the pious people with good sight, with solid legs, with good health, surrounding Christ, speaking of high matters, the kingdom to come, and the mysteries of the Scriptures, turning on Bartimaeus and saying, "What, can't you keep quiet? Your eyes, your eyes, what do they matter whilst speaking of God?" Bartimaeus was like someone jumping out of context to ask God for something he needed desperately while some ceremonial is going on, and destroying the good harmony. He would be thrown out immediately. He would be silenced. But the Gospel says also that, in spite of all these people who wanted to shout him down, he insisted because it mattered so much to him. The more they tried to silence him, the more he shouted.

Here is my message. There is a saint of Greece called Maxim, a young man, who went to church one day and heard the reading of the Epistle in which it says that we should pray unceasingly. It struck him in such a way that he thought he could do nothing else than fulfil this commandment.

He walked out of the church, went into the neighbouring mountains and set out to pray unceasingly. Being a Greek peasant of the fourth century, he knew the Lord's Prayer and some other prayers. So he proceeded, as he tells us, to recite them, again and again and again. Then he felt very well. He was praying, he was with God, he was elated, everything seemed to be so perfect, except that gradually the sun began to go down and it became colder and darker, and as it became darker he began to hear all sorts of worrying sounds—cracking branches under the paws of wild beasts, flashing eyes, sounds of smaller beasts being killed by larger beasts, and so forth. Then he felt that he was really alone, a small, unprotected thing in a world of danger, of death, of murder, and that he had no help if God didn't give it. He no longer continued saying the Lord's Prayer and the Creed; he did exactly what Bartimaeus did, he began to shout "Lord Jesus Christ, Son of God, have mercy on me". And he shouted like that all the night because the creatures and the flashing eyes didn't give him a chance to go to sleep. Then the morning came and he thought, because all the beasts had gone to sleep, "Now I pray", but by then he felt hungry. He thought he would collect some berries and he started towards a bush, but then he realised that all those flashing eyes and savage paws must be hidden somewhere in the bushes. So he began to make his way very softly and at every step said "Lord Jesus Christ, save me, help me, help me, save me. O God, help me, protect me", and for every berry he collected he had certainly prayed several times.

Time passed and after many years he met a very old and experienced ascetic who asked him how he had learnt to pray unceasingly. Maxim said "I think it's the devil who taught me to pray unceasingly." The other man said "I think I understand what you mean, but I would like to be sure that I understand you right". Maxim explained how he had gradually become accustomed to all these noises and dangers of the day and night. But then temptations came upon him, temptations of the flesh, temptations of the mind, of the emotions, and later more violent attacks from the devil. After that there was no moment day or night when he did not shout Godwards, saying "Have mercy, have mercy, help, help, help". Then one day after fourteen years of that, the Lord appeared to him; and the moment the Lord appeared, stillness, peace, serenity came on him. There was no fear left—of darkness or of bushes, no fear of the devil—the Lord had taken over. "By then" Maxim said "I had learned that unless the Lord Himself comes, I am hopelessly and completely helpless. So even when I was serene and peaceful and happy I went on praying 'Lord Jesus Christ, Son of God, have mercy on me'," because he knew that only in the divine mercy was there any peace of heart and peace of mind and stillness of body and rightness of will.

So Maxim learnt to pray not in spite of the turmoil, but because of the turmoil, and because the turmoil was a real danger. If we could be aware that we are in much greater turmoil, that the devil is lurking, trying to catch and destroy us, that every human meeting is judgment, is crisis, is a situation in which we are called either to receive Christ or to be Christ's messenger to the person whom we are meeting, if we realised that the whole of life has this intensity of meaning, then we would be able to cry and to pray continuously, and turmoil would be not a hindrance but the very condition which teaches us to pray while we are still too inexperienced to pray from the depth without any prompting, without any incitement into prayer.

When we know nothing about prayer, when we have not prayed at all in our lives or not enough, how can we learn to pray in the conditions of life in which we live? I have experimented on that in a variety of situations: in the years when I was in medical work, five years in the war, in the priesthood and so forth, and it does work. It does work if you are simple enough to do it. It works in this way.

Awake in the morning and the first thing you do, thank God for it, even if you don't feel particularly happy about the day which is to come. "This day which the Lord has made, let us rejoice and be grateful in it." Once you have done this, give yourself time to realise the truth of what you are saying and really mean it—perhaps on the level of deep conviction and not of what one might call exhilaration. And then get up, wash, clean, do whatever else you have to do, and then come to God again. Come to God again with two convictions. The one is that you are God's own and the other is that this day is also God's own, it is absolutely new, absolutely fresh. It has never existed before. To speak in Russian terms, it is like a vast expanse of unsoiled snow. No one has trodden on it yet. It is all virgin and pure in front of you. And now, what comes next? What comes next is that you ask God to bless this day, that everything in it should be blessed and ruled by Him. After that you must take it seriously, because very often one says "O God, bless me", and having got the blessing we act like the prodigal son—we collect all our goods and go to a strange country to lead a riotous life.

This day is blessed by God, it is God's own and now let us go into it. You walk in this day as God's own messenger; whomever you meet, you meet in God's own way. You are there to be the presence of the Lord God, the presence of Christ, the presence of the Spirit, the presence of the Gospel—this is your function on this particular day. God has never said that when you walk into a situation in His own Name, He will be crucified and you will be

103

the risen one. You must be prepared to walk into situations, one after the other, in God's name, to walk as the Son of God has done: in humiliation and humility, in truth and ready to be persecuted and so forth. Usually what we expect when we fulfil God's commandments is to see a marvellous result at once—we read of that at times in the lives of the saints. When, for instance, someone hits us on one cheek, we turn the other one, although we don't expect to be hit at all, but we expect to hear the other person say "What, such humility"—you get your reward and he gets the salvation of his soul. It does not work that way. You must pay the cost and very often you get hit hard. What matters is that you are prepared for that. As to the day, if you accept that this day was blessed of God, chosen by God with His own hand, then every person you meet is a gift of God, every circumstance you will meet is a gift of God, whether it is bitter or sweet, whether you like or dislike it. It is God's own gift to you and if you take it that way, then you can face any situation. But then you must face it with the readiness that anything may happen, whether you enjoy it or not, and if you walk in the name of the Lord through a day which has come fresh and new out of His own Hands and has been blessed for you to live with it, then you can make prayer and life really like the two sides of one coin. You act and pray in one breath, as it were, because all the situations that follow one another require God's blessing.

A number of years ago I spoke about this at Taizé, and I have remained in correspondence with about thirty of the boys and girls there. One of them wrote to me and said "I have tried your advice. I have tried it with all my energy. I have not yet had a minute in which I was not praying and acting, praying and acting, and now I can't hear the word of God, I can't bear this sort of prayer." I said to her "You've got indigestion. You should have used common sense in prayer, as one uses common sense in life. You cannot, having never prayed before, start with eighteen hours of dialogue and prayer with God continuously like this while you do other things. But you can easily single out one or two moments and put all your energy into them. Simply turn your eyes Godwards, smile at Him and go into it. There are moments when you can tell God 'I simply must have a rest, I have no strength to be with You all the time', which is perfectly true. You are still not capable of bearing God's company all the time. Well, say so. God knows that perfectly well, whatever you do about it. Go apart, say for a moment 'I'll just have a rest. For a moment I accept to be less saintly'."

In this way we can just rest and look at things which are also God's things—trees and buildings—and then after a while we go back to Him. If we try to pray continuously, we will be defeated quite soon; but if we choose moments intelligently we can do it.

If you do that you will be able to pray. You can experiment, but don't forget to be sober because there is a sin which the Spiritual Fathers call "spiritual greed", which consists of wanting to have more and more of God at a moment when you should be put on a diet and have just a little and enough for you.

MANAGING TIME

IN the tense modern life which we live, the problem of managing time is an all important one. I am not going to try to convince you that you have plenty of time and can pray if you want to; I want to speak of managing time within the tensions, the rush of life. I will spare you any description of the way in which one can make time: I will only say that if we try to waste a little less of it, there will be more of it. If we use crumbs of wasted time to try to build short moments for recollection and prayer, we may discover that there is quite a lot of it. If you think of the number of empty minutes in a day when we will be doing something because we are afraid of emptiness and of being alone with ourselves, you will realise that there are plenty of short periods which could belong both to us and to God at the same time. But what I want to speak about is something which I believe is more important. It is the way in which we can control and stop time. We can pray

107

to God only if we are established in a state of stability and inner peace face to face with God, and these things release us from the sense of time—not objective time, the kind we watch—but the subjective sense that time is running fast and that we have no time left.

First of all I would like to draw your attention to something which we all know and we all discuss. There is absolutely no need to run after time to catch it. It does not run away from us, it runs towards us. Whether you are intent on the next minute coming your way, or whether you are completely unaware of it, it will come your way. The future, whatever you do about it, will become the present, and so there is no need to try to jump out of the present into the future. We can simply wait for it to be there, and in that respect we can perfectly well be completely stable and yet move in time, because it is time that moves. You know the situation when you are in a car or on a train and you sit back, if you are not driving, and you look out of the window; you can read, you can think, you can relax, and yet the train moves, and at a certain moment, what was the future, whether it is the next station or the last station to which you are going, will be present. I think this is very important. The mistake we often make with our inner life is to imagine that if we hurry we will be in our future sooner—a little like the man who ran from the last carriage of the train to the first, hoping that the distance between London and Edinburgh would be shortened as a result. When it is that kind of example we see how absurd it is, but when we continually try to live an inch ahead of ourselves, we do not feel the absurdity of it. Yet that is what prevents us from being completely in the present moment, which I dare say is the only moment in which we can be, because even if we imagine that we are ahead of time or ahead of ourselves, we are not. The only thing is that we are in a hurry, but we are not moving more quickly for this. You must have seen that more than once. Someone with two heavy suitcases, trying to catch a bus, rushes: he is as quick as he can be, he runs as fast as the suitcases allow, and he is all intent on being where he is not.

But you know what happens when we

take a walk on holiday. We can walk briskly, gaily and quickly, or if we are of the right age and condition, we can even run, but we don't feel in a hurry at all, because what matters at that moment is the running, not the arriving. This is the kind of thing we must learn about prayer, to establish ourselves in the present. Usually we think or we behave as though the present was an imaginary line, very very thin indeed, between the past and the future, and we roll from the past into the future, continually passing this line in the same way as you can roll an egg on a cloth. If you do this, it runs continuously, it is nowhere at any moment, there is no present, because it is always in the future.

Not everyone is lucky enough to have decisive experiences, "disclosure situations", which teach him things, but I would like to tell you in a few words about a very useful experience which I had.

During the German occupation of France I was in the resistance movement and, coming down into the Underground, I was caught by the police. This is one of the most interesting experiences I have had. Leaving aside all the romantic trimmings as to what happened and how it happened, I will put it in more philosophical terms concerning time. What took place at that moment was this: I had a past, I had a future, and I was moving out of one into the other by walking briskly down the steps. At a certain moment someone put a hand on my shoulder and said "Stop, give me your papers." At that moment several things happened. For one thing, I began to think very quickly, feel very intensely, and to be aware of the whole situation with a relief and a colourfulness which I had never before perceived on the last steps of Metro Etoile. The second thing was that I realised that I had no past, because the real past I had was the thing for which I should be shot. So, that past was not there any more. The false past which I was prepared to talk about had never existed, and so I found myself standing there like the lizard who had been caught by the tail and had run away leaving the tail somewhere behind, so that the lizard ended where the tail had been. Then I discovered another thing which was very interesting (though I did not elaborate so much on the philosophy of time at that moment) but what I perceived

111

at once, and what I understood gradually, is that you have a future only to the extent to which you can foresee a minute before it happens, or an inch before you reach it, what will come next—i.e. nothing is coming next because you have no idea of what could come—you are like someone standing in an unknown room in the dark. You stand there and all that's there is darkness pressing on your eyes. There may be nothing ahead of you or infinity ahead of you, it is all the same thing. You end exactly where darkness begins. So I discovered that I had no future either. It was then I discovered that living in the past on the one hand and in the future on the other hand was simply not possible. The lizard had no tail, and darkness was on my face. I discovered that I was pressed into the present moment, and all my past, that is, all the things that could be, were condensed in the present moment with an intensity, a colourfulness that was extremely exhilarating and which allowed me eventually to get away!

Now as far as time is concerned, there are moments, without going into so much detail, when one can perceive that the present moment is there, the past is irremediably gone—it is irrelevant except to the extent to which it is still in the present —and the future is irrelevant because it may happen or it may not. That happens for instance, when you are in an accident, when you are at a moment of danger which requires extremely quick action. You have no time to roll comfortably from the past into the future. What you have got to do is to be so completely in the present that all your energies and all your being are summed up in the word *now*. You discover with great interest that *you* are in the *now*. You know the very, very thin plane which geometry teaches us has no thickness. This geometric plane which has absolutely no thickness, which is "now", moves along the lines of time, or rather time runs under it, and brings to you "now" everything you will need in the future. This is the situation we must learn, and we must learn it in a more peaceful way. I think we must do exercises in stopping time and in standing in the present, in this "now" which is my present and which is also the intersection of eternity with time.

What can we do? This is the first exercise. It can be done at moments when you have absolutely nothing to do, when nothing pulls you either backward or forward and when you can use five minutes, three minutes or half an hour for leisure and for doing nothing. You sit down and say "I am seated, I am doing nothing, I will do nothing for five minutes", and then relax, and continually throughout this time (one or two minutes is the most you will be able to endure to begin with) realise, "I am here in the presence of God, in my own presence and in the presence of all the furniture that is around me, just still, moving nowhere." There is, of course, one more thing you must do: you must decide that within these two minutes, five minutes, which you have assigned to learning that the present exists, you will not be pulled out of it by the telephone, by a knock on the door, or by a sudden upsurge of energy that prompts you to do at once what you have left undone for the past ten years. So you settle down and say "Here I am", and you are. If you learn to do this at lost moments of your life when you have learned not to fidget inwardly, but to be completely calm and happy, stable and serene, then extend the few minutes to a longer time and then to a little while longer still. A moment will come, of course, when you will require some defences, because you can sit quietly for two minutes even if the telephone does ring or someone knocks at the door, whereas fifteen minutes may be too long for either the telephone to ring or for the person to stand at the door. But then make up your mind that if you were not at home you would not open the door, nor would you answer the telephone. Or, if you have more courage, or are more convinced of what you are doing, you can do what my father did. He had a little note on the door saying "Don't go to the trouble of knocking. I am at home but I will not open the door." This is a way which is much more decisive, because people understand it at once, whereas if you say "Kindly wait five minutes", the kindness usually dies out within two minutes!

Then when you have learned this stability, this serenity, you will have to learn to stop time not only at moments when it drags or has stopped anyway, but at moments when it rushes, when it puts forward claims. The way to do it is this. You are doing something which you feel is useful; you feel that unless this is done the world will falter on its course; and then if at a certain moment you say "I stop", you will discover many things. First, you will discover that the world does not falter and that the whole world—if you can imagine it—can wait for five minutes while you are not busy with it. This is important, because we usually deceive ourselves, saying "Well, I must do it: it is charity, it is duty, I cannot leave it undone." You can, because at moments of sheer laziness you will leave it undone for much longer than the five minutes you have chosen. So the first thing you say is: "Whatever happens, I stop here." The simplest way to do it is to have an alarm clock. Wind it and say "Now I am working without looking at the clock until it rings." That is very important; one of the things which we must unlearn, is looking at the clock. If you are walking somewhere and are aware that you are late, you look at your watch. But you cannot walk as quickly while you look at your wrist as if you simply look straight ahead. And whether you are aware that it is seven

116

minutes or five or three minutes, you are nonetheless late. So add a starting time and you will be there on time, or else if you are late, walk as fast and as briskly as you can. When you are at the door, have a look to see how contrite you must look when the door is opened! Then, when the alarm clock goes off, you know that for the next five minutes the world has come to an end and you will not move from the spot. It is God's own time and you settle back in His own time quietly, silently and peacefully. In the beginning you will see how difficult it is, and you will feel that it is of great importance that you should finish, say, writing a letter or reading a paragraph. In reality, you will discover quite soon that you can very well postpone it for three, five or even ten minutes and nothing happens. And if you are doing something that requires attention, you will discover how much better and more quickly you can do it.

I will give you another example. In the beginning, when I was a physician, I felt it was most unfair to the people who were in the waiting room if I was slow in seeing the person who was with me in the consulting room. So the first day I tried to be as quick as I could with those in the consulting room. I discovered by the end of my surgery hours that I had not the slightest recollection of the people I had seen, because all the time a patient was with me, I was looking beyond him with clairvoyant eyes into the next room and counting the heads of those who were not with me. The result was that all the questions I asked I had to ask twice, all the examinations I made I had to make twice or even three times. When I had finished, I could not remember whether I had done these things or not. Of course everyone is not like me; you may be able to recollect much better than I, but this is just an example of what may happen even to one of you.

Then I felt this was simply dishonest, and I decided that I would behave as if the person who was with me was the only one who existed. The moment I began to feel "I must be quick", I would sit back and engage in small talk for a few minutes just to prevent myself from hurrying. I discovered within two days that you no longer need to do anything like that. You can simply be completely concerned with the person or task that is in front of you, and when you have finished, you will discover that you have spent half the time doing it, instead of all the time you took before; yet you have seen everything and heard everything.

Since then I have often given this kind of advice to many people in a variety of walks of life, and it works. So if you do these exercises, beginning with stopping time that is not moving, and ending with time that is trying to move fast, and you stop and say "no", you will discover that the moment you have overcome the inner tension, the inner agitation, the fidgeting and the anguish, time passes perfectly well. Can you imagine that only one minute goes by every minute? That is exactly what happens. It is strange, but it is true, though from the way we behave one might think that five minutes could rush past in thirty seconds. No, every minute counts as much as the next minute, every hour as much as the next hour. Nothing disastrous happens at all. You may say "Shall I have time to do it all?" I will answer you in a very Russian way: "If you do not die first, you will have time to do it. If you die before it is done, you don't need to do it." There is another saying of the same kind which you can keep for future reference: "Do not worry about death. When death is there, you are no longer there, but as long as you are there, death is not." It is the same principle. Why should I worry about a situation which will resolve itself?

Once you have learned not to fidget, then you can do anything, at any speed, with any amount of attention and briskness, without having the sense of time escaping you or catching up with you. It is like the feeling I spoke of, when you are on holiday, with all your holiday ahead of you. You can be quick or slow, without any sense of time, because you are only doing what you are doing, and there is no purpose. And then you will see that you can pray in every single situation in the world, that there is no situation which can prevent you from praying. What *can* prevent you from praying is that you allow yourself to be in the storm, or you allow the storm to come inside you instead of raging around you.

You may remember the story in the Gospel of the storm on the Sea of Galilee: Christ asleep in the boat and the storm raging around. At first the apostles work hard and hopefully in order to survive. Then at a certain moment they lose heart, and the storm that was outside comes inside —the storm is within them too. Anguish, death no longer simply circle round, they come inside. And then they turn to Christ and do what we very often do with God: we look at God in time of stress and tragedy, and we are indignant that He is so peaceful. The story in the Gospel underlines it by saying that Christ was sleeping with His head on a pillow—the final insult. They are dying and He is comfortable. This is exactly what we feel about God so often. How dare He be blissful, how dare He be so comfortable when *I* am in trouble? And the disciples do exactly what we do so very often. Instead of coming to God and saying "You are peace, you are the Lord, say a word and my servant will be healed, say a word and things will come right", they shake Him out of His sleep and say "Don't you care that we are perishing?" In other words, "If you can do nothing, at least don't sleep. If you can do nothing better, then at least die in anguish with us." Christ reacts, He gets up and says "Men of little faith!" and brushing them aside, He turns towards the storm and, projecting His inner stillness, His harmony and peace on the storm He says "Be still, be quiet" and everything is quiet again.

This we can do, and we must be able to do it. But it requires systematic, intelligent training, in exactly the same way as we train to do other things. Learn to master time, and you will be able—whatever you do, whatever the stress, in the storm, in tragedy, or simply in the confusion in which we continuously live—to be still, immobile in the present, face to face with the Lord, in silence or in words. If you use words, then you can bring to God all that is around you, all the storm. If you are silent, you can rest in the "eye" of the cyclone or the hurricane, in the calm there, but leaving the storm around you to rage, while you are where God is, at the only point of total stability. But this point of total stability is not a point where nothing happens. It is the point where all the conflicting tensions meet and are counter-balanced by one another and are held in the powerful hand of God.

Real silence is something extremely

intense, it has density and it is really alive. I remember a passage from the lives of the desert saints in which one of them was asked by his brothers to deliver a spiritual discourse for the benefit of a bishop who was to visit them, and he said "No, I won't because if my silence doesn't speak to him, my words will be useless." This is the kind of silence we should try to learn about, or to learn to achieve. How can we do it? What I can try to direct you to is a parable or an image, that of birdwatching.

If we want to watch birds in their stirring in the woods or the fields, we must be awake before them. We must be prepared to be alert, alive, completely out of sleep before the first bird wakes. Indeed, before the birds are aware that morning has come. We must go into the fields or into the woods and settle there absolutely still, absolutely silent, absolutely relaxed, so that we should never stir and frighten the light sleepers which are around us, because otherwise they will make their way into the distance and fly off where we can neither hear nor see them. Birdwatching implies on the one hand this stillness, this quiet, this repose, and at the same time an intense alertness, because if you sit in the fields dreaming the undreamt dreams of your short night, all the birds will have gone long before you realise that the sun is warming your back. It is essential to be alert and alive, and at the same time still and relaxed, and this is contemplative preparation for contemplative silence; this very difficult balance between the kind of alertness that will allow you with a completely open mind, completely free from prejudice, from expectation, to receive the impact of anything that will come your way, and at the same time this stillness that will allow you to receive the impact without dreaming into it the picture of your own presence that will be destructive of it.

About twenty years ago, soon after my ordination, I was sent before Christmas to an old people's home. There lived an old lady, who died some time later at the age of 102. She came to see me after my first celebration and said "Father, I would like to have advice about prayer." So I said "Oh yes, ask So-and-so." She said "All these years I have been asking people who are reputed to know about prayer, and they have never given me a sensible reply, so I thought that as you probably know nothing, you may by chance blunder out the right thing." That was a very encouraging situation! And so I said "What is your problem?" The old lady said "These fourteen years I have been praying the Jesus Prayer almost continually, and never have I perceived God's presence at all." So I blundered out what I thought. I said "If you speak all the time, you don't give God a chance to place a word in." She said "What shall I do?" I said "Go to your room after breakfast, put it right, place your armchair in a strategic position that will leave behind your back all the dark corners which are always in an old lady's room into which things are pushed so as not to be seen. Light your little lamp before the ikon that you have and first of all take stock of your room. Just sit, look round, and try to see where you live, because I am sure that if you have prayed all these fourteen years it is a long time since you have seen your room. And then take your knitting and for fifteen minutes knit before the face of God, but I forbid you to say one word of prayer. You just knit and try to enjoy the peace of your room."

She didn't think it was very pious advice but she took it. After a while she came to see me and said "You know, it works." I said "What works, what happens?" because I was very curious to know how my advice worked. And she said "I did just what you advised me to do. I got up, washed, put my room right, had breakfast, came back, made sure that nothing was there that would worry me, and then I settled in my armchair and thought 'Oh how nice. I have fifteen minutes during which I can do nothing without being guilty!' and I looked round and for the first time after years I thought 'Goodness, what a nice room I live in—a window opening onto the garden, a nice shaped room, enough space for me, the things I have collected for years'." Then she said "I felt so quiet because the room was so peaceful. There was a clock ticking but it didn't disturb the silence; its ticking just under-lined the fact that everything was so still and after a while I remembered that I must knit before the face of God, and so I began to knit. And I became more and more aware of the silence. The needles hit the armrest of my chair, the clock was ticking peacefully, there was nothing to bother about, I had no need of straining myself, and then I perceived that this silence was not simply an absence of noise, but that the silence had substance. It was not absence of something but presence of something. The silence had a density, a richness, and it began to pervade me. The silence around began to come and meet the silence in me." And then in the end she said something very beautiful which I have found later in the French writer, Georges Bernanos. She said "All of a sudden I perceived that the silence was a presence. At the heart of the silence there was He who is all stillness, all peace, all poise."

After that she lived for about ten more years and she said that she could always find the silence when she was quiet and silent herself. This does not mean that she stopped praying; it means that she could sustain this contemplative silence for a while, then her mind began to quiver and she turned to vocal prayer until the mind was still and settled again, then she dropped out of words into silence as before. Very often this could happen to us—if instead of being so intent on doing things, we could simply say "I am in God's presence, what a joy, let us be still."

In the life of a Catholic priest of France, the Curé d'Ars, Jean Baptiste Vianney, there is a story of an old peasant who used to spend hours and hours sitting in the chapel motionless, doing nothing. The priest said to him "What are you doing all these hours?" The old peasant said "I look at Him, He looks at me and we are happy."

This can be reached only if we learn a certain amount of silence. Begin with the silence of the lips, with the silence of the emotions, the silence of the mind, the silence of the body. But it would be a mistake to imagine that we can start at the highest end, with the silence of the heart and the mind. We must start by silencing our lips, by silencing our body in the sense of learning to keep still, to let tenseness go, not to fall into daydreaming and slackness, but to use the formula of one of our Russian saints, to be like a violin string, wound in such a way that it can give the right notes, neither wound too much to breaking point, nor too little so that it only buzzes. And from then onwards we must learn to listen to silence, to be absolutely quiet, and we may, more often than we imagine, discover that the words of the Book of Revelation come true: "I stand at the door and knock."

In the next chapter we will consider the basic conditions for establishing prayer in connection with addressing God and being able to speak to Him.

ADDRESSING GOD

IN this chapter I would like to say something about the moment when we are so disposed that prayer becomes really possible and live. In view of what I have said before and the assumptions that have been constantly present in the background, prayer is obviously a relationship, an encounter, a way in which we have a relationship with the living God. There is a moment when this relationship becomes something live. And since it is a question of relationship, I want to start with something that refers equally to prayer and to human relationships.

A relationship becomes personal and real the moment you begin to single out a person from the crowd. That is when this person becomes unique in his own right, when he ceases to be anonymous. Someone has spoken of "the anonymous society" in which instead of having names and surnames and qualities and personality, we are defined in general terms like "the ratepayers", and so forth. In our relationships with people there is very often this element of anonymity: "they". We speak in the third person when we feel that someone can easily be replaced by someone else, because the relationship is functional, not personal, and this *function* can be fulfilled by someone else, while this *person* would not be replaceable by anyone else. In other languages I would have said that a relationship becomes real the moment when one begins to think of a person in terms of "thou" instead of "you". It does not require a change of language, it is an inner change. You know very well, I am sure, that one can have this "I" and "thou" relationship or an "I" and "it" relationship with someone.

Prayer begins at the moment when, instead of thinking of a remote God, "He", "The Almighty", and so forth, one can think in terms of "Thou", when it is no longer a relationship in the third person but in the first and second persons. Take, for instance, the Book of Job, where there is a conflict. Take so many other instances in Scripture and in life, in the lives of saints and sinners, when there was tension and a violent confrontation. This is always a personal thing. There is no prayer as long as there is a cautious, distant and chilly relationship, as long as there is ceremonial between us and God, as long as we cannot speak to Him but must go through a long and complex series of words and actions. But there is a moment when, instead of all this, we pierce through and speak in the first and second person. We say "I" and we expect Him to be "Thou", or "You" in the singular. Let it not be the polite, the royal "You" but the singular and unique "You."

And then there is another moment in a warm human relationship: the moment when we look for a name for a person. I am not speaking now of a general surname empty of meaning, but of when we begin to see how this person relates to a name. You know, for instance, how personal in a positive and also a negative way a nickname can be. A nickname may be a way of crushing you down, of ruling you out, of destroying everything there is between two people; but it may also be a name which only two people use, or a very small group of persons, who are so deeply and so intimately linked to each other that the name is filled with meaning for them, because it is supremely personal. The more absurd it is, in a way, the more personal it is, because no one else would invent it except you.

Then there is the surname. The surname often seems to us to be alien, a general term like "humanity"; so many people have the same surname. And yet if we look at it more attentively in human relationships, we can realise that the surname is the mark of a community. From generation to generation back in history, people who are of our blood, whose life is within our bones, within our heredity, within our minds, have had this name, and this name links us back very far to generations of people and will probably link us forward to others, and by the various links of marriage and family will constitute a vast network of people deeply connected with each other. If, instead of thinking of surnames, you think of heredity, of genealogy, is it not what we find in two of the Gospels concerning the Lord? Is this not the very thing which this genealogy points to: a link from generation to generation with concrete, real human beings? So a surname is something that we can treat with immense interest, because it holds all our past in one word, and if we thought of other people in these terms, surnames could themselves come to life. Instead of being an expression of someone's uniqueness and of his uniqueness in his relationship with us, as is a nickname, it would link us all of a sudden to this unique person, to a whole world of beings . . .

Then there is the Christian name, the name which we receive in baptism: it is the name by which God takes possession of the person. The Christian name links the person with God, because as he receives it he dies with Christ and rises again, but also it links him with a variety of people who have been granted this same name, and first of all with the one who made a pagan name into a Christian name, the first saint who brought it to the Church.

We also have another name, one which we do not know. You remember the passage in the Book of Revelation which says that in the Kingdom each will receive a white stone with a name written on it, a name which is known only to God and to him who receives it. This is no nickname, no family name, no Christian name. It is a name, a word, that is exactly identical with us, which coincides with us, which *is* us. We may almost say it is a word which God pronounced when he willed us into existence and which is us, as we are it. This name defines our absolute and unrepeatable uniqueness as far as God is concerned. No one can know the name, as no one can, in the last analysis, know anyone as God knows him; and yet it is out of this name that everything else comes that can be known about us.

You may be wondering why I am concentrating on names. It is because part of our prayer is related directly to God and is our personal link with Him, but another part of our prayer is our link with the whole outside world, and when we pray for each other, when we pray for the world, we are bringing to God names and nothing else. But these names are full of meaning or empty of meaning according to circumstances, according to whether or not we are able to sense the depth of what we say. If we name people before God without any sense of name, simply using names as labels, empty of depth, our relationship is of poor quality; if we pronounce a name with any of the significance I have tried very briefly to express, then our prayer becomes not only a bringing forth of a person on our open hands, as it were, but it links us to this person with a depth not of compassion, not of love, but of identification, sharing, solidarity, which has quite a different quality.

This is also true in the other direction. Unless we can find the right name for God, we have no free, real, joyful, open access to Him. As long as we have to call God by general terms like "The Almighty," "The Lord God", as long as we have got to put "the" before the word to make it anonymous, to make it a generic term, we cannot use it as a personal name. But there are moments when the sacred writers, for instance, burst out with something which has the quality of a nickname, something which no one else could possibly say, which is at the limit of the possible and the impossible, which is made possible only because there is a relationship. Remember the psalm in which, after more restrained forms of expression, suddenly David bursts out, "You, my Joy!" That is the moment when the whole psalm comes to life. Saying

"O Thou our Lord", "O You are the Almighty", and the like, was stating to God facts about Him, but bursting out and saying "O You my Joy!" was quite a different thing. And when we can say to God "O You my Joy!" or when you can say "O You the pain of my life, O You who are standing in the midst of it as torment, as a problem, as a stumbling block!", when we can address Him with violence, then we have established a relationship of prayer.

And so it is very important for us to have a look and find out whether there are names in our experience that apply to God. For one thing, the use of names may change from time to time. There are moments when we perceive one aspect of our relationship with God, and at other times we see other aspects, exactly in the same way in which, in friendly or affectionate relationships with each other, we do not choose one single expression for speaking to one another, but a variety of shades and nuances. We have "The Almighty", we have "The Lord", we have "The Creator", we have "The Provider", we have "Wisdom", but we also have a very simple name like Jesus, which is, shall I say, a Christian name.

It may sound rather strange to say that Christ has a Christian name, and I hope you will understand what I mean. It reminds me of a discussion which one of my parishioners, who is a Christian, had with her husband, who is not. He spent forty years of his life trying to give her evidence that Christianity is worthless, and one day, in desperation, she said "How *can* you say that, when God was first of all a Jew and then became a Christian?" The way in which I say that Jesus is a Christian name may remind you very much of this very primitive approach, yet it is a human name, the first Christian written in the roll of the Church. And if we remember this, if we become aware of the closeness it establishes between Him and us, then we will understand why generations of Christians have fastened on this name; probably not because St. Paul says "At the Name of Jesus every knee shall bow", for though it is certainly true, it is not this which makes a name warm, lovable. That would be tantamount to speaking of "The Almighty" or "The Lord", but the name of Jesus is a live, real, personal name.

And you may find many other names. I am quite certain that if some day "O Thou my Joy!" or any other cry of this kind bursts out of you, it will be the moment when you will have discovered a relationship between Him and you which is your own, which is not a relationship that you share with many other people. I do not mean to say that you should not share it. We have words for God which belong to all of us, but there are words that belong only to me or to you in the same way in which, in human relationships, there are surnames, there are Christian names, there are nicknames. It is good if you can have a nickname by which you can call the Almighty God, a nickname that has all the depth of your heart, all the warmth you are capable of; it becomes your way of saying "In my uniqueness this is the way I perceive your uniqueness."

If in the process of discovering where you stand in relation to God—how far you are an outsider—you come to the point of knocking, of going deeper and deeper into yourself, turning your prayer *on yourself,* bringing yourself to the point where there *is* a door to knock on, the point where it *can* be opened—there *will* come a moment when the door *will* open, but then you must have a name for God. You must be able to say a word that shows that it is *you* who have been in search of Him, and not just an interchangeable human being in quest of an anonymous God.

In the process of searching you will have endured pain, anguish, hope, expectation —all the range of human emotions. God will have been the desired One and He will have been the frustrating One. He will have been the One you long for and the One you hate because He escapes you, the One you love beyond everything, without whom you cannot live, and whom you cannot forgive, because He does not respond, and many other things. And out of this search there will gradually emerge words which you can speak to God out of your own experience of the quest of the Grail, words which are your own. You may discover that they coincide with many words which others have used. Then they will cease to be anonymous words; they will be words which you have in common with other people but which have become truly yours. But do not use words which are in the common dictionary, words which do not belong to you. When you begin to hear a chain rattling on the door, when you have a feeling that it will open, then come out with the words which are your own and call God by the name which He has won in your own life. At that moment you will have met. In the ever deepening and enriching relationship that follows, you will have a great deal of time to discover other words, to discard the words of hatred and anguish. Like the martyrs spoken of in the Book of Revelation, you will say "Thou hast been just and true in all Thy ways" (Rev. 15:3). And these words then will wipe out all the words of bitterness, all the names that sound cruel; but you will keep names which are personal, which are your own, and which will be a real relationship and a real way of being related to the living God.

What I have said about "learning to pray" is, I think, practical enough so that you can experiment. Quite obviously there is a great deal more that should have been said about the same things and a great deal more that one should say about other things, but do try to experiment along the lines I have suggested and you will see that it is not a waste of time. Search for a name, and if you have no name, do not be surprised that no one hears you: you are not calling.

TWO MEDITATIONS

The Mother of God

THERE are two types of ikons of the Mother of God.

The usual type is that which you find in East and West—the Virgin holding the child. This is an image of several things and not only the Mother of God as a person. It is an image of the Incarnation, an assertion of the Incarnation and its reality. It's an assertion of the true and real motherhood of the Virgin. And, if you look attentively at the ikon, you will see that the Mother of God holding the Child never looks at the Child. She always looks neither at you nor into the distance but her open eyes look deep inside her. She is in contemplation. She is not looking at things. And her tenderness is expressed by the shyness of her hands. She holds the Child without hugging Him. She holds the Child as one

143

would hold something sacred that one is bringing as an offering, and all the tenderness, all the human love, is expressed by the Child, not by the mother. She remains the Mother of God and she treats the child, not as baby Jesus, but as the Incarnate Son of God who has become the son of the Virgin and He, being true man and true God, expresses to her all the love and tenderness of man and God both to His mother and to His creature. This is one image.

Another image, which you find very seldom, is the image of the Mother of God alone, without the obvious presence of Christ. I will describe just one of them. It is a Russian ikon of the 17th century. You see a Russian peasant girl who has lost her veil, whose hair, parted in the middle just falls down on a rather square face. Her eyes are big and she is looking into infinity or into the depths. Certainly not a view of anything which is in front of her. If you look more you see two hands. Two hands that couldn't be where they are simply because anatomy wouldn't allow it. They are not there to be part of a realistic picture, they are there to express what neither the face nor the hands nor the eyes could express without ceasing to express something more important. They are hands of anguish. And then, in the corner of the ikon, almost invisible, pale yellow on pale yellow background, a little mount and an empty cross. This is the mother contemplating the crucifixion and death of her only begotten Son.

When we turn to the Mother of God in prayer, we should realise more often than we do that any prayer we offer to the Mother of God means this: "Mother, I have killed thy Son. If you forgive me, I can be forgiven. If you withhold forgiveness *nothing* can save me from damnation." And it is amazing that the Mother of God, in all which is revealed in the Gospel, has made us understand, and made us bold to come to her with this very prayer, because there is nothing else we can say. To us she is the Mother of God. She is the one who brought God Himself into our earthly situation. In that sense we insist on this term "Mother of God". Through her God became Man. He was born into the human situation through her. And she is not to us simply an instrument of the Incarnation.

She is the one whose personal surrender to God, her love of God, her readiness to be whatever God wills, her humility in the sense in which I have spoken about it to you already, is such that God could be born of her. There is, in one of our great saints and theologians of the 14th century, a passage on the Mother of God in which he says "The Incarnation would have been as impossible without the 'Here am I, the handmaid of God' of the Virgin, just as it would have been impossible without the will of the Father." Here there is a total cooperation between her and God. Speaking of the Incarnation and the attitude of the Blessed Virgin, I think an English writer has put it in a remarkable way—Charles Williams in his novel *All Hallows Eve*. He says of the Incarnation that what makes its uniqueness is that "one day a virgin of Israel was capable of pronouncing the sacred name with all her heart, all her mind, all her being, all her body, in such a way that in her word became flesh". I think this is a very good theological statement that signifies the place which she has in the Incarnation.

We love her, we feel perhaps in her in a

peculiar way we see the Word of God spoken by Paul who says "My power is made manifest in weakness." We can see this frail virgin of Israel, this frail girl, defeating sin in her, defeating hell, defeating everything by the power of God which is in her. And this is why at moments like persecutions, when indeed the power of God is made manifest in nothing but weakness, the Blessed Virgin stands out so miraculously, so powerfully in our eyes. If she could defeat earth and hell then we have in her a tower of strength and one who can intercede and save, and we mark the fact that in her there is no discrepancy with the will of God, that she is in perfect harmony with Him, by using a formula of prayer which we use only for God and for her, "Save us". We don't say "Pray for us".

Staretz Silouan

In 1938 a man died on Mount Athos*. He

---

* A book has been written about his life: Archimandrite Sofrony, *The Undistorted Image*, trans. by Rosemary Edmunds, The Faith Press 1958.

was a very simple man, a peasant from Russia who came to Mount Athos when he was in his twenties and stayed for about fifty years. He was a man of utmost simplicity. He had gone to Athos because he had read in a pamphlet about the Holy Mountain that the Mother of God had given a promise that anyone who would serve the Lord in these monasteries, she would stand for him and pray for him. So he just abandoned his village and said "If the Mother of God is prepared to stand for me, there I go, and her business is to save me." He was a most remarkable man and for a long time he was in charge of the workshops of the monastery. The workshops of the monastery were manned by young Russian peasants who used to come for one year, for two years, in order to make some money, really farthing added to farthing, in order to go back to their villages with a few pounds, perhaps, at the utmost to be able to start a family by marrying, by building a hut and by buying enough to start their crops. One day other monks, who were in charge of other workshops, said "Father Silouan, how is it that the people who work in your workshops work so well while you never supervise them, while we spend our time looking after them and they try continuously to cheat us in their work?" Father Silouan said "I don't know. I can only tell you what I do about it. When I come in the morning, I never come without having prayed for these people and I come with my heart filled with compassion and with love for them, and when I walk into the workshop I have tears in my soul for love of them. And then I give them the task they have to perform in the day and as long as they will work I will pray for them, so I go into my cell and I begin to pray about each of them individually. I take my stand before God and I say 'O Lord, remember Nicholas. He is young, he is just twenty, he has left in his village his wife, who is even younger than he, and their first child. Can you imagine the misery there is there that he has had to leave them because they could not survive on his work at home. Protect them in his absence. Shield them against every evil. Give him courage to struggle through this year and go back to the joy of a meeting, with enough money, but also enough courage, to face the difficulties'." And he said "In the beginning I prayed with tears of compassion for Nicholas, for his young wife, for the little child, but as I was praying the sense of the divine presence began to grow on me and at a certain moment it grew so powerful that I lost sight of Nicholas, his wife, his child, his needs, their village, and I could be aware only of God, and I was drawn by the sense of the divine presence deeper and deeper, until of a sudden, at the heart of this presence, I met the divine love holding Nicholas, his wife, and his child, and now it was with the love of God that I began to pray for them again, but again I was drawn into the deep and in the depths of this I again found the divine love. And so," he said, "I spend my days, praying for each of them in turn, one after the other and when the day is over I go, I say a few words to them, we pray together and they go to their rest. And I go back to fulfil my monastic office."

Here you can see how contemplative prayer, compassion, active prayer, are an effort and a struggle, because it was not just saying "Remember, O Lord, him, him and him." It was hours and hours spent just praying with compassion, praying with love, both blending together.